AFRICAN UHURU

THE FIGHT FOR AFRICAN FREEDOM IN THE RISE OF THE GLOBAL SOUTH

Roger McKenzie

To the Leader

"African Uhuru"
The fight for African freedom in the rise of the Global South
Roger McKenzie

First Published in 2024 by Manifesto Press

MANIFESTO PRESS CO-OPERATIVE |
Decolonising the labour movement series

Manifesto Press
Ruskin House
23 Coombe Road
Croydon CR0 1BD

TYPESET IN *ARBORIA* AND *PLANTIN MT PRO*
DESIGNED AND ILLUSTRATED BY **CORATA GROUP**

ISBN 978-1-907464-61-4

The moral rights of the author have been asserted

studio@manifestopress.coop

manifestopress.coop

CONTENTS

Introduction
– African history and the rise of the Global South

The power of history is inescapable. To begin to understand the move towards a more multipolar world we must be clear about how we have arrived at this point.

This point is the unstoppable rise of the Global South.

One of the key reasons for our arrival at this moment is the role that Africans, both on the continent and across the diaspora, have played in helping to create this transitional moment in world history.

From the outset it is important to accept that people of African descent have always resisted racism.

Resistance to racism began the moment racism did. Africans have never been passive victims of racism with just the occasional heroic uprising to our name.

African history did not begin with the transatlantic slave trade. There was a thriving and rich history centuries before the Europeans arrived on the continent.

But this brutal and most vicious system of trade in human beings helped to spawn the anti-Black racism that we see today.

Unintentionally, for the slavers and colonialists, the racism they created also gave birth to a culture of resistance that has helped Africans to play a leading, though not solitary, role in the rise of the Global South and its breaking of the Eurocentric power over the planet.

The argument I set out in this book is that African resistance has historically meant challenging

Eurocentrism through both a collective and individual resistance to racism as part of working-class and peasant communities.

The Eurocentric world is dying. It has choked to death on its own militaristic arrogance.

The key question is what will replace it? Will it be another even more authoritarian new era that continues the United States doctrine of full spectrum dominance? Or will it be a new multipolar world where the term sovereignty is not weaponised and respect is a genuine two-way street?

Africans have long been key drivers of revolutionary thought but where this has not been completely ignored it has in practice been barely recognised.

Nevertheless, Africans will be key to the future invigoration of socialist national, regional and international movements as we move towards a more multipolar world.

In past struggles Africans have drawn on the lessons of the fights against enslavement, colonialism and violent racist attacks. This will be repeated going forward.

Africans have found strength in the creation of communities of resistance to help to move towards African freedom – African Uhuru – because the logic of the benefits of collective action against racism has been apparent from when the first Africans rose up and fought back against enslavement and exploitation.

This book will demonstrate that negative portrayals of Africans are entirely wrong. It is part of an ongoing attempt to dehumanise Africans and to paint them as a people who require being saved from starvation and wars and who are simply incapable of independent thought or action.

This will require de-centring Europe as the dominant world view and the way the labour and socialist movement operates in the Global North.

My aim is to undo the lingering and pervasive impacts of colonialism and to challenge the notion that Europe is the font of all knowledge and the legitimate yardstick against which everything else should be measured.

This book aims to look at the role played by Africans in the rise of the Global South through the prism of Britain and the British Empire.

Another book will be required to concentrate more on the vast African continent itself and the role played by Asians in challenging the existing world order.

Language is important and there are some deliberate choices made in this book.

I mainly use the term Africans throughout this book. When I use the term Black I am generally referring to people of African and Asian descent but make it clear if I am using it differently.

Black is never used here in a descriptive sense but in the spirit of the legendary former editor of *Race and Class*, A. Sivanandan, who once said: "Black is not the colour of our skin. It is the colour of our politics."[1]

I use the term Global South throughout the book as a

---

1. A. Sivanandan, 'From Resistance to Rebellion: Asian and Afro-Caribbean Struggles in Britain', *Race and Class*, Pamphlet No 10, The Institute of Race Relations, London, 1986.

political project aimed at developing unity of oppressed nations rather than as a geographic description.

When I speak of Europe I include the European-dominated settler colonial regimes such as the United States, Australia and, of course, Israel.

These are places where the indigenous populations were deliberately destroyed or where people were enslaved so that Europeans could access the land, resources and the cheap or free labour of what remained of the people.

To manage this discussion this book is arranged in four chapters.

The first chapter looks at theories of African self-liberation and in particular the role of Pan-Africanism as being a key driver of resistance.

Chapter two looks at how Africans have united in Britain to organise resistance to racism within and outside of the labour and trade union movement.

The third chapter explores some African examples of building international solidarity and the importance that this default position of transnationalism plays in African liberation strategies.

This chapter looks at the central roles played in African liberation by the Communist International, the Universal Negro Improvement Association and the Non-Aligned Movement.

The fourth and final chapter looks to the future and sets out the contribution that Africans are making towards building a multipolar world and socialism.

This section also examines the role of international structures such as the African Union, the United

Nations and the BRICS plus bloc – pioneered by Brazil, Russia, India, China and South Africa – in contributing towards building cross-national African solidarity.

I am clear throughout this book that the labour movement of the Global North has not done enough to support people of African descent in the fight against racism and must significantly up its game including challenging its own deep-seated Eurocentrism and prejudices.

In arguing this all the errors in this book are entirely mine but the opportunity to win this new multipolar world is the responsibility of us all.

We have a World to win!

Anonymous, *Third Pan-African Congress in Lisbon*, May 1923

CHAPTER ONE
The Radical Tradition of African self– Liberation

Introduction
– The Radical Tradition of African Liberation

There is an African radical tradition of resistance to racism that stretches from beyond the continent of Africa to include the entire African diaspora.

The very notion of a radical African tradition of resistance – as distinct from any general forms of radicalism – raises two fundamental objections from its critics.

Firstly, there is the (arguably racist) contention that Africans are simply incapable of creating distinct philosophical or theoretical works comparable to anything derived from a European tradition.

And secondly, there is the very sophisticated argument that engaging in a distinct tradition based on "blackness" only serves to legitimise false theories of race.

It also brings together the rich variety of attitudes and beliefs that characterises people of African, African-Caribbean and Asian descent under a convenient but, nevertheless, false umbrella.

The first of these contentions is a characteristic of notions of white supremacy. The notion of white supremacy, in a British context, owes its lineage to the British Empire and so-called scientific writings that were used to justify and perpetuate racial superiority over the colonised.

The industry of justification was not only used to tell the colonised how inferior they were to their masters. It was also an industry of perpetuation. This took place on two fronts.

Firstly, it was to continue to manufacture the idea of white supremacy with the general public in Britain as well as the next generation of colonisers.

Without popular support for the notion of white supremacy and the "true believers" to continue the process, the second point, convincing the lawmakers and business to maintain the necessary financial resources, would have been much more difficult to achieve.

The problem is that the mere ending of the British Empire did not end the racist ideology that had been manufactured over many years.

Racism in Britain, by the state and in the workplace must be seen as a legacy of colonialism where centuries of white supremacist beliefs and actions have left a network of stereotypes and prejudices.

Put simply, imperialism was sustained by notions of superiority which it is impossible, if they so desired, to wipe out overnight. These beliefs, having had so much invested in them, still seep through every layer of British society today.

The stereotypical views of Black women and men as lacking the intelligence of white people comes from views manufactured during colonial rule.

The justification for the racial discrimination that can still be seen in the British jobs market, where Black workers are around three times as likely to be unemployed as compared to their white counterparts, also finds its heritage in the Empire.

Racism is a relatively modern invention whilst slavery, as an institution, has been well documented since the biblical times. But, racism was never an established doctrine.

Rather, gender, religion and culture, as well as, of course, class, seemed to be the dominant reasons for discrimination in the Ancient Greek and Roman times.

Race and Class

To even suggest the existence of a Black or African radical tradition of resistance is to immediately force a rethink of the radical traditions that developed in Europe.

The discussion below on tradition and on Marxist conceptions of African self-liberation contributes towards that discourse.

Marxism is an indispensable tool in grasping the complexity of racism and African self-liberation as a form of resistance.

It is indispensable because it highlights the relation of racism to capitalist modes of production and it also recognises and illustrates the crucial role played by racism in the capitalist economy.

There are at least four basic views of racism in the Marxist tradition.

The first attempts to subsume racism within a catch-all of working-class exploitation. Those who argue this rather fundamentalist view of life tend to ignore racism not determined by the workplace and not a purely economic relationship.

The second view acknowledges the importance of racism within the workplace (for example, job discrimination and wage differences between Black and white workers) but remains silent about these operations outside of the workplace.

Those taking this view suggest that Black workers of African or Asian descent are subjected both to general working-class exploitation and to a specific "super-exploitation" resulting from less access to jobs and lower wages.

This view accents a more intense struggle against racism but seems to limit the resistance to racism in the workplace.

The third view is the so-called "Black Nation thesis".

This is a view that has been most influential among Black Marxists, particularly in the United States.

This view claims that the operation of racism is best understood as relating to specific working-class exploitation alongside national oppression.

Here, it is claimed, people of African descent constitute an oppressed national minority.

The basis of this outlook is the definition of nation put forward by Stalin in his *Marxism and the National Question* (1913). Stalin argued that:

"...a nation is a historically constituted, stable community of people formed on the basis of a common language, territory, economic life and psychological make-up manifested in a common culture".[2]

This introduces an important cultural dimension that appears to have been overlooked by the Marxist account of racism mentioned above.

---

2. J.V Stalin, *Marxism and the National Question*, Foreign Languages Publishing House, Moscow, 1913.

The linking of racism to nations (or peoples) dominating others provides an important consideration for the resistance strategies that might be adopted by those being dominated. It narrows what might naturally be seen as a starting point for the alliance-building necessary to resist racism.

The Garveyist movement of the post-First World War era, which I discuss in more detail below, forced African radicals to understand the importance of the cultural dimension to the resistance to racism.

The Garveyist brand of nationalism – even with its later conservative and pro-capitalist agenda – appeared to take cultural concerns more seriously than many Marxists did.

The fourth view in the Marxist tradition suggests racism results not only from working-class exploitation but also from xenophobic attitudes that cannot be simplistically reduced to class exploitation.

Here, racist attitudes have a life and logic of their own although heavily influenced by psychological factors and cultural practices. The primary motivation for those arguing this line was an opposition to the influence that the Black Nation thesis was having on the white and African left internationally.

These conceptions of racism reveal the importance of a clear understanding of the relationship between race and class.

Put simply, are class considerations more important than race or is the opposite the case? The same debate occurs when considering other key factors such as gender and sexuality.

Michael Zweig (2005) provided a helpful contribution to the debate when he suggests that:

"Class, race and gender are different but not wholly separate; there is no experience of class that is not inflected by race and gender, and no experience of gender or race that is not inflected by class."[3]

Also Lustig (2004) argues that:

"It would be a mistake to reduce race to class. But it would also be a mistake we see, to try to understand it without class. Race is a political and economic, and not just a cultural and psychological phenomenon".[4]

The Eurocentric nature of the class narrative is a major problem.

Cedric Robinson provided a critique of Western Marxist theory in the excellent book *Black Marxism* (1983).

Robinson said Marxism was: "…a Western construction – a conceptualisation of human affairs and historical development which is emergent from the historical experiences of European peoples mediated, in turn, through their civilization, their social orders, and their cultures.

"Certainly its philosophical origins are indisputably Western."[5]

I am not suggesting for a moment that the basic construct of historical materialism is anything other than sound and, indeed, a vital tool for us to utilise.

3. M. Zweig, 'Class as a Question in Economics' in J. Russo and SL Linkon (eds) *New Working-Class Studies*, Cornell University Press, Ithaca, 2005, p.109.

4. R.J. Lustig, 'The Tangled Knot of Race and Class' in M. Zweig (ed) *What's Class Got to do with it?*, Cornell University Press, Ithaca, 2004, p.53.

5. C. Robinson, *Black Marxism: The Making of the Black Radical Tradition*, Zed Press, London, 1983, p.2.

It is still clearly the best scientific method of understanding the society in which we live. However, to merely subsume the life, experiences and traditions of African workers under the class narrative only provides a very partial picture.

CLR James, the great Trinidadian intellectual and activist, made a penetrating analysis on the interrelationship of class, race and gender. Writing in the Trotskyist *Resolution on the Negro Question* (1939) James said:

> "The awakening political consciousness of the negro (sic) not unnaturally takes the form of independent action uncontrolled by whites.

> "The negro (sic) has long felt that more than ever today the urge to create their own organisations under their own leaders and thus to assert not only in theory but in action, their claim to complete equality with other American citizens."

James added: "Such a desire is legitimate and must be vigorously supported even when it takes the form of a rather aggressive chauvinism."[6]

James was breaking with the view that African workers, as a minority, had to be led by progressive white organisations, be they the Communist Party, which had a strong anti-colonialist – though not always anti-racist – stance in Britain, or white radicals of good, liberal intentions.

The important thing to take from the work of James was that African workers, wherever they found themselves in

---

6. C.L.R. James, 'The SWP and Negro Work', *SWP New York Convention Resolutions*, 11 July 1939, https://www.marxists.org/archive/james-clr/works/1939/07/negro-work.htm , accessed 2 May 2024.

the world, were capable of and should create their own organisations under their own leaders. It was, and is, a powerful argument for African self-liberation.

James had foreseen this not through some supernatural power but by applying sound historical methods based on how African workers had always resisted racism.

CLR James

In providing an intellectual underpinning for African self-liberation, James drew no distinction between those which might exist within existing structures, such as trade unions or political parties, and those that might be formed outside.

The important thing here is to recognise that African self-liberation outside of the labour and trade union movement does not necessarily represent a formation antagonistic towards the ideals of collectivism.

The intersection between race and class is central to this book. The placing of Black self-liberation or organised groups within the trade union movement in Britain strengthens this intersection of race and class rather than diminishes it.

Legendary US Communist Gus Hall described African self-organised formations in trade unions as "a vitally necessary form of struggle".[7]

Hall also argued that arguments against these communities of resistance in trade unions as being divisive were arguments used by trade unionists that were content with the status quo and saw the activity that came from these African self-organised formations as rocking the boat.[8]

Hall believed these self-liberation groups stimulated African worker activity as well as that of white workers against racism.

African self-liberation is, in his opinion, critical for bringing about a Black working-class alliance,

---

7. G. Hall, *Fighting Racism: Unity for Equality, Justice, Trade Unionism, Democracy, Peace*, International Publishers, New York, 1985, p.141.

8. Hall, *Fighting Racism*, p.141.

an alliance that would influence the rest of the trade union movement to tackle exploitation in the workplace and in communities.[9]

In *Black Marxism* Cedric Robinson uses the example of three intellectual giants, Richard Wright, CLR James, and Du Bois, to illustrate how the Black radical tradition developed.

Du Bois, in particular, played a leading role in the Pan-African Congress movement, as I explain below.

W.E.B. Du Bois

9. Hall, *Fighting Racism*, p.149.

The Pan-African Congress was an example of a successful early twentieth century transnational Black radical movement.

Perhaps more than anyone Du Bois was responsible for the establishment of a transnational African radical tradition.

If Du Bois could be credited with being the father of the transnational African radical tradition then James can be assigned the role of family elder, particularly for his influence on Caribbean African radicalism.

James is cited by the leaders of the Grenadian New Jewel Movement revolution of 1979 as being a key influence.

However, there is little doubt that James was one of the leading intellectual figures behind African radicalism in Britain. This radical influence was central to African self-liberation within and outside of the trade union movement.

The contribution made by James to the development of the African radical tradition across the Caribbean and in Britain was immense.

James is another example of how the experience of British colonial rule, allied to an understanding of the role of African workers in the working class as a whole, was used to inform the resistance of racism in Britain.

Others from the Caribbean such as Claudia Jones, originally from Trinidad and Walter Rodney from Guyana also successfully straddled the line between activist and intellectual. They are important examples, along with James, of the transnational nature of African resistance.

The movement of these intellectual-activists was more than just about physical travel, it was a transference of ideas, cultures and the traditions of resistance to racism. The wider availability of travel for African workers during the twentieth century merely serves to underline the transnational nature of Black resistance.

Pan-Africanism

Pan-Africanism will be key to the development of the new multipolar world. But what is Pan-Africanism and how can it help us today?

Like so many philosophies it is far too often lazily portrayed as a singular approach and if we are to de-centre or decolonise the European view of the socialist and Labour movement then we must understand more about this central foundation of African thought.

Pan-Africanism is a movement by and for people of African descent. Its aim has always been to create a unity of thought and action between Africans whether they are on the continent or anywhere in the diaspora.

Rooted in the anti-slavery and anti-colonial movements, Pan-Africanism dates back to the nineteenth century but there are competing approaches that spring from its foundation.

It is also not the only belief system within the African liberation movement.

It should also be no surprise that there is more than one vision for African liberation.

Far too often – even on the left – Africa is treated as a country rather than a vast continent of some 1.2 billion people spread over 11.5 million square miles with at least 3000 native languages.

The divisions, already present on the continent, were only multiplied as the colonial powers drew lines to create 54 countries without any regard for history or culture.

Some claim that the founding of Pan-Africanism can be traced back to the important writings of formerly enslaved people such as Ottobah Cugoano and Olaudah Equiano.

Others see Edward Willmott Blyden and James Africanus Beale Horton as the true founders of Pan-Africanism in their writings, during the height of European colonialism, about the necessity for African nationalism and self-determination.

Pan-Africanism has never been just a male pastime – although it is clear there are some Black men who would have you believe otherwise in their mistaken belief in a dominant African patriarchy.

There is plenty of evidence to confirm the matriarchal dominance in many African societies.

Women also played a key role in the early development of Pan- Africanism. Alice Kinloch and Jeanne Nardal played foundational roles as did the work later of Amy Ashwood, Amy Jacques Garvey and Alma La Badie.

Their work acted as a solid base for a new generation of Pan-Africanists at the turn of the twentieth century, including JE Casely Hayford, and Martin Robinson Delany (who was responsible for coining the phrase "Africa for Africans" which was later adopted by Marcus Garvey).

But there is no doubting the importance to the development of the Pan-Africanist movement of the great African American Marxist academic and activist William Edward Burghardt Du Bois.

Du Bois was one of the driving forces behind the groundbreaking Pan-African Conference held at Westminster Town Hall in London during July of 1900.

Around 50 participants at the conference focused on the bitter struggle against racism in the United States, Britain, the West Indies and in the African colonies.

Key to the discussions were the calls for the end of colonialism, the need for self-determination and the demand for political rights.

There were to be no further Pan-Africanist gatherings until 1919 when the first Pan-African Congress took place at the Grand Hotel in Paris.

First Pan-African Congress

Again Du Bois was the key organising driving force behind this and a subsequent series of PACs in London, Paris, and New York in the first half of the twentieth century.

The interwar years gatherings were heavily influenced by communism and trade unionism. We can see this through the writing and activities of Marxists Du Bois,

George Padmore, Paul Robeson and the great trade unionist Isaac Wallace-Johnson.

During this period a younger group of Pan-Africanists – notably Aimé Césaire, Cheikh Anta Diop, Leopold Sedar Senghor and Ladipo Solanke – all became part of a growing movement for African freedom and founded the new philosophy of "Negritude."

Negritude essentially reclaims the value of being African as well as the importance of celebrating the rich diversity of the continent's culture.

After World War II, Pan-Africanism became increasingly focused on ending colonialism. Some of the leading Pan-Africanists migrated back to Africa. Padmore and Du Bois both made Ghana their home.

This coincided with a new wave of Pan-Africanists being foregrounded in the movement to replace the largely US, British and West Indian-based activists.

Kwame Nkrumah, Sekou Ahmed Toure, Ahmed Ben Bella, Julius Nyrere, Jomo Kenyatta, Amilcar Cabral and Patrice Lumumba all came to the forefront of the freedom movement as revolutionary leaders.

All led movements to win power from the former colonial rulers. They were all also subjected to interference, and in some cases overthrow, from their former colonial powers acting at the behest of the US during the Cold War period.

The 1960s saw the growth of a new movement called Afrocentrism. Rooted in African nationalism, recognising the importance of the continent in a similar vein to Pan-Africanism, this movement centres the history of African people over non-African civilisations.

Followers of this view say Black Africans have been written out of history or, at best, discredited and that this was a key part of the legacy of both slavery and colonialism.

Some critics dismiss Afrocentrism as a version of Eurocentrism but with a black face.

As we look back on the development of Pan-Africanism we can see that as travel opportunities widened and modes of communications developed then so did the movement grow.

The opportunities for more people of African descent to travel and the widened access to new electronic means of communication and the means to produce literature has sparked a new growth in the Pan-African movement.

The international movement for reparations for the inhumane treatment of Africans during the transatlantic slave trade and colonialism has been a point of unity between the full range of African political philosophies – of which only a handful have been mentioned here.

But key Pan-African developments are also taking place with the trade union movement.

The Global African Workers Institute was set up in 2018 at a major conference in London.

GAWI brings together leading trade unionists from across the African diaspora to coordinate the actions of Black trade unionists against the twin assault of neo-liberal globalisation and the rise of far-right authoritarianism.

During its London launch the 100 strong delegates were clear that these vicious assaults undermine democracy, incite misogyny, ignore the climate emergency and increase global inequality which all leads to what GAWI describes as an era of "global apartheid."

The latest GAWI meeting, the third in-person after London and Abuja in Nigeria in 2019, like the Nigerian gathering, came immediately after the conference of the International Trade Union Confederation - Africa.

Chaired by the International President of the Coalition of Black Trade Unionists, Terry Melvin and the outgoing General Secretary of ITUC-Africa, Kwasi Adu-Amankwah, the meeting shared regional updates from the US, Canada, Haiti, Europe, Sudan, Eswatini, Niger and Nigeria.

There was also a report on work across the globe to organise domestic workers, many of whom are Black workers and mainly women.

The meeting then explored how GAWI could bring added value to the work of trade unionists on the continent and importantly how the struggles of trade unionists of African descent from the continent and across the diaspora can be united to provide a fresh impetus to the struggle for African freedom from racism and new forms of colonialism.

These are exciting times for Pan-Africanism. The fight to end the pillage of the African continent by the former colonial powers is taking on a new momentum as is the movement to defeat the deep-seated and often denied racism that is the everyday experience of most Black people.

We are able to continue this fight because of very brave women and men who went before us. Our history gives us the strength to continue.

Summary

It would be thoroughly misleading to suggest that everyone, whatever the colour of their skin, is in favour of African self-liberation within trade unions (or anywhere else for that matter).

I have shown that many arguments put forward by opponents of Black self-liberation strategies in trade unions are based on racist rhetoric. Many of these views are derived from historically received notions of supremacy or designed to mask an unwillingness or inability to resist racism.

At the heart of the tapestry of theories that come together to form African self-liberation or communities of resistance in trade unions is whether and how best to resist racism.

There is no one form of resistance to racism that takes place on its own. The reality is that a combination of approaches takes place depending on the particular circumstances.

The point of unity for Black workers is the shared experience of racism in Britain alongside the common heritage of colonial rule and resistance.

I am not suggesting that all Black working-class activity must be seen solely within the prism of the trade union movement or any other specific collectively organised formation.

I show that even though there are multi-influences on the formation of African self-liberation with British trade unions and political parties, and that even while some of these influences, such as Black nationalism or Afrocentrism, are inherently conservative, they retain an element of radicalism that has provided both a tension and edge to these formations.

Essentially, however, Black self-organisation in trade unions in Britain has a direct lineage to the black radical tradition described by Robinson and others such as Robin Kelley.

Aside from the Black workers who helped to found the British trade union movement, Black immigrants to the country from 1919 did not arrive as blank slates. They were, in the same way that Kelley describes Black Communists in Alabama:

".....born and reared in communities with a rich culture of opposition"[10]

The resistance to racism by Black workers in the workplace, or not, through self-liberation groups or individually, is a well-concealed yet central part of the history of the British working class.

It is a history that needs to be re-told so that the tradition and methods of resistance can be passed on to the next generation to continue the struggle against racism.

Chapter two looks at how this African resistance to racism played out in the belly of the beast itself – in Britain.

---

10. R.D.G. Kelley, *Hammer and Hoe: Alabama Communists during the Great Depression*, University of North Carolina Press, Chapel Hill, North Carolina, 1990, p.99.

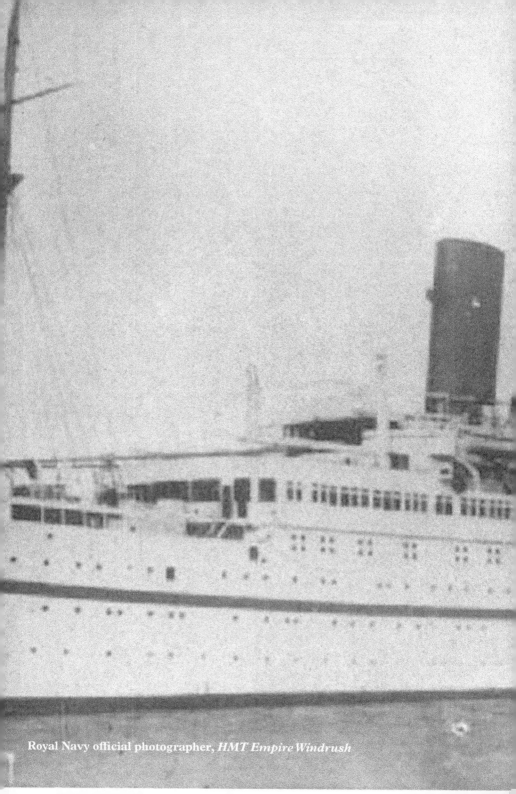

Royal Navy official photographer, *HMT Empire Windrush*

CHAPTER TWO

Communities of resistance in the belly of the beast

Introduction

Africans resisted racism through communities of resistance in Britain and across the British Empire.

The resistance is often portrayed as being as a result of attacks that took place against Africans but, in reality, the fight back against racism and the building of power was constant as well as both collective and individual in its character.

There were constant acts of resistance to racism in workplaces wherever Africans were to be found. This included the sabotage of equipment – to slow down the production process – as well as larger more obvious acts of defiance such as strikes.

This chapter concentrates on periods as well as collective acts of African resistance that were pivotal in the African liberation movement in Britain and in other parts of the diaspora.

The "Red Summer" of 1919

The summer of 1919 was as red in Britain as it was on the other side of the Atlantic in the United States.

It was a year of international unrest and fear at the same time as being a time of excitement, hope and radicalism springing from the new world that had been ushered in by the 1917 Russian Revolution.

Much of Britain's 1919 Black population was made up of seafarers, dock workers and colonial troops returning from doing their duty in World War I.

This should not be taken to conclude that Black workers only arrived in Britain after World War I. Far from it. There has been a sizeable Black population in Britain since Roman times when soldiers of African descent were sent to guard Hadrian's Wall.

But 1919 witnessed a new phenomenon – organised attacks on a community in Britain based on race.

Not only were there major racist attacks in almost every port in Britain where there were African people but these uprisings also took place across the US.

Some 65 towns and cities across the US saw deadly racist attacks against African Americans.

Red Summer 1919 JS

The widespread nature of the uprisings suggests that something more profound was taking place in 1919 than unconnected incidents of racism.

More workers were migrating across borders after the great imperialist war had ended which led to a wider use of the new system of international passport controls – which only really started during the war.

The introduction of passports was, of course, destined to be an object used to regulate the movement of some rather than others.

In post-war Britain the African community, whether born in the country or not, were liable to be stopped by the police and expected to produce identification, which might include a passport, or face prosecution.

This targeting of the African community went alongside troops returning from their war duties with resentment and bitterness over the scarcity of employment and directed their frustrations and hostilities against the Black workers.

Accusations of "stealing" whites' jobs were accompanied by the tiresome and seemingly age-old charges of African men "stealing" white women from white men – as if women were property.

The reality was that most members of the African workforce in Britain lost their positions to the returning white veterans.

The plight of returning African veterans was ignored and went largely unrecorded.

The reality was that the circumstances for many Black people were so dire that large swathes of the

Black community that had the means to do so chose to leave Britain.

Most of the newer immigrants, however, if questioned, considered themselves British subjects, because that was indeed their legal status, and chose, when possible, to remain in Britain.

Economic depression and the accompanying unemployment were persistent and serious problems in the interwar period and were most acutely felt by Britain's working classes – Black or white.

But the usual divide and rule card was played by the ruling classes to divert attention away from the rampant exploitation of the working class.

African workers were labelled as the ones responsible for all the ills facing the white working class.

This all came to a head in 1919 as African families were attacked in their own homes, at work and in the streets around the towns and cities where they lived.

Most of the Black population of Britain was concentrated in Liverpool, South Wales and London. These areas were already being portrayed by the gutter press in terms such as "distinct foreign colonies," and in clear racist terms, in one Liverpool newspaper, as "partly a check against the pollution of a healthy community by undesirables."

The scale of the attacks on the Black population in Britain was astonishing in their ferocity and their scale.

African people literally had to flee for their lives and choose where they were going to make a stand to protect their lives.

It was a lesson learned from slavery and colonialism
– where battles had to be chosen and collective
resistance built.

But whilst there were always some individual white
collaborators in standing up against racist attacks, there
is little evidence of any widespread organised resistance
by the white left of 1919 in making common cause with
Black workers against the vicious assaults that were
taking place.

But racism also emerged in other ways.

Racism was often acute in those workplaces where
African and white workers mixed – particularly on the
docks. But even where there was not "racial mixing" in
workplaces racism, from white employers or supervisors,
was a fact of everyday life.

But African people also experienced racism in this period
in securing services that they needed just to survive.

They could not readily access banking, decent housing
or use social amenities, such as local pubs and clubs,
where they were often barred by the proprietors or
because of the danger it posed by being on what might
be considered "white turf."

The emergence of visible Black professional and student
populations were met by a societal colour bar whose
inherent racist and discriminatory practices also affected
their prospects for progress.

For the growing African community how to stand up
racism became an increasingly important issue and, in
some cases, a matter of life and death.

To simply be in the wrong place at the wrong time could
all too easily cost you your life.

The lesson from both enslavement and colonialism was that whilst individual acts of resistance to racism had its place and was a frequent choice for African people, self-liberation through collective resistance was the order of the day.

If unions and the left were missing in action on behalf of African workers then new institutions needed to be formed within both workplaces and in communities.

African workers organised their own informal banking systems, worked together to provide accommodation for each other and organised their own entertainment in each other's homes or friendly premises – although both were liable to police and racist attacks.

In the workplace the African community began to self-organise on both an informal and formal basis.

The formal self-liberation formations in the pre-World War II 1930s led to organisations such as the League of Coloured Peoples, the Coloured Seamen's Union and the Coloured Film Artistes Association.

Black Resistance on the Front Line

As I have shown (above), Black workers were predominantly, though not exclusively, found in the major ports of the UK.

While there has been an African population in Britain since Roman times it grew substantially during World War I, when colonial workers were shipped over to Britain to work in munitions factories and on the merchant ships.

Prior to World War I trade unions in Britain took the principled position of resisting moves by employers to pay Black workers, African or Asian, less than their white counterparts.

But this principled position disappeared after the War even though unions in the colonies sought to forge an alliance with them against these racist employer practices.

There is little evidence to suggest why this change in attitude took place within the unions.

After all, the establishment of a low paid strata of workers within a sector could only serve to hold down the wages of all workers as African and white workers are pitted against each other.

One can only assume that the pressure by returning servicemen, complaining of African workers "stealing their jobs" forced the hand of the unions to change policy.

In Britain during this period, African seamen stood alongside whites in the quest for trade union recognition and higher wages in ports such as Cardiff, Liverpool and London.

Having served and died in their hundreds on British merchant ships as they helped to keep Britain's maritime lifeline open there was an assumption by these African workers that this shared struggle and sacrifice would at least be recognised by wages and labour conditions on a par with native-born white English seamen.

Any notion that these African workers could join in common cause was quickly forgotten by their white comrades in the post-war scramble for jobs.

For the first time African seafarers as a group found themselves being verbally and physically attacked on the street, with a venom which had previously been reserved for the Chinese and Lascars.

It was clear which way the wind was blowing when the British trade union movement proposed the institution of a British-first hiring policy.

This policy conceded that many "coloured" seamen were indeed British and had a right to work, but called for preference to be given to white Britons. Meanwhile the government sought the means to repatriate West Indian seamen who were now considered surplus to requirements.

Under the terms of the Alien (Coloured Seamen) Order of 1925, West Indian and African seafarers were required to register with the authorities as aliens, unless they could produce satisfactory documentary proof of British nationality.

Even in cases where African and Asian seafarers had such documentation the local authorities often ignored it and forced them to register as aliens.

This racist onslaught on the part of both government and union continued until the late 1930s and drastically reduced the number of African seafarers from the Caribbean in the British mercantile marine. It was only with the onset of World War II that the demand for their labour would revive once more.

The reasons for the pivotal role played by African seafarers from the Caribbean in shaping political consciousness in African communities throughout the Atlantic World, as well as at home in the Caribbean, are complex.

It is possible that an island culture builds a certain commitment to the sea.

But, the relatively high literacy rate among the African working class (courtesy of the excellent education provided by the British Empire) in the islands by the end of the nineteenth century, in contrast with other parts of the world, was also an important factor.

This meant that African seafarers from the Caribbean often had both the inclination and the skills to not only go to sea but also to stand up for their legal and/ or political rights in whatever context they found themselves in because of their exposure to racism and the tradition of resistance where they lived.

Most importantly, however, may have been the attitude or world view they carried with them.

African seafarers from the Caribbean tended to combine the internationalist, cosmopolitan perspective of the independent labour-migrant with a strong identification with the Caribbean.

Evidence of the latter may be seen in the fact that many sent money back to families left at home in the Caribbean despite absences stretching into years, or dreamed of returning to the islands at some future date.

St Lucian Nobel laureate Derek Walcott alludes to this dream in his epic poem *Omeros*, as he evokes and encapsulates the elements of Caribbean identity.

In the final analysis, then, culture, society and identity in the Caribbean islands cannot be understood without reference to the sea:

let the deep hymn
of the Caribbean continue my epilogue;
may waves remove their shawls as my mourners walk home
to their rusted villages, good shoes in one hand,
Passing a boy who walked through the ignorant foam,
and saw a sail going out or else coming in,
and watched asterisks of rain puckering the sand.[11]

Derek Walcott

While much of the resistance to racism by African workers during the interwar years was individual acts of defiance and self-defence, the period also witnessed the emergence of a number of important African communities of resistance.

11. D. Walcott, *Omeros*, Faber and Faber, London, 2002, Chapter LXIV:I.

These groups, while primarily formed to advocate for African workers on a range of social issues, such as housing, inevitably also became involved in matters more directly related to the workplace.

Some of the most important of these groups were student-based, such as the West African Students' Union, the Union for Students of African Descent and the Gold Coast Students Association.

These groups were all concerned with the wide range of student welfare matters surrounding their education but increasingly became involved in wider political affairs. This was particularly the case with those that became involved in anti-imperialism campaigns.

These were relatively small and largely middle-class groups. Aside from those African workers that found themselves in Britain in the aftermath of World War I, the financial resources for international travel and lodgings were simply not available to those of working class or peasant stock.

These organisations still, however, merit some attention to be paid to their activities and influence.

Colonial Seamen's Association

The Colonial Seamen's Association (CSA) was founded in 1935 as a response to the racist 1935 British Shipping (Assistance) Act.

The Act subsidised the British shipping industry by safeguarding seamen's jobs – as long as they were white – during the brutal economic depression of the 1930s.

One of the requirements for payment of the subsidy from the Act was that the ship employed only "British seamen."

This led to many ship owners sacking all but their white seafarers.

In an act of collective resistance by African, Chinese and South Asian seamen the CSA was formed to campaign against the Act.

With opposition to the Act not confined to local campaigners, with opposition to the new rule also coming from the Colonial Office and the India Office, the discriminatory provision was eventually removed in March 1936.

One of the key campaigners against the Act was Chris Braithwaite.

Born in Barbados in 1885, Chris Braithwaite was a sailor, a docker, and a Communist.

Braithwaite joined the British Merchant Navy as a teenager and sailed the world. He lived in Chicago for a while, but during World War I rejoined the Merchant Navy.

After the war, he moved to London to work for the Shipping Federation.

Because of his political activity Braithwaite often used the name Jones to avoid victimisation by his employer and could never rely on his union, the National Union of Seamen (NUS) for support.

The NUS was part of the process of gaining employment on ships so there was no alternative than to become a member. But the NUS was well-known amongst African seafarers for its racism.

Even during the Red Summer of 1919 (see above) the NUS colluded with the ship owners to victimise any Black seamen who they accused of any involvement in the resistance to the attacks that took place.

In 1930, Braithwaite joined the newly formed Seamen's Minority Movement (SMM) a Communist Party of Great Britain (CPGB) rank and file group. It was through this group, which I will discuss more below, that Braithwaite became one of the founders of the CSA.

Chris Braithwaite

Braithwaite had an international outlook and was involved in supporting anti-racist causes around the world. Through his maritime links he was even involved in smuggling weapons to Ethiopia to aid the resistance to the invasion of the country by the fascist forces of Benito Mussolini.

His transnational anti-racism work widened the links of the SMM and laid bare the racism that existed at the time within the NUS.

The League of Coloured Peoples

The League of Coloured Peoples (LCP) was founded in 1931 by Harold Moody. The LCP, which grew to become the pre-eminent national political organisation for African people in Britain during the 1930s and 40s, became most involved in raising awareness of the very high levels of unemployment within the Black community (particularly amongst African seamen).

The LCP also lobbied politicians about the racism faced by African commissioned officers during the Second World War and exposed the killing of civilians during the Italian invasion of Abyssinia.

Moody, born in Kingston, Jamaica in 1882, qualified as a doctor at Kings College, London in 1910. He, with a small committee of fellow activists, founded the LCP at a meeting at the Central YMCA in Tottenham Court Road, London on March 13 1931.

Moody was elected the first President (he was to be the only President of the organisation during its existence). The LCP was highly significant because it was, according to Ramdin "the first major black organisation which aimed to bring the black races together".[12]

Eventually the LCP could boast that it had male and female officers coming from places such as West Africa and Ceylon (now Sri Lanka) as well as Jamaica (including the great journalist Una Marson).

CLR James and the great West Indian cricketer and politician Learie Constantine were also associated with the LCP.

The initial aims of the LCP were to:

- Promote and protect the social, educational, economic and political interests of its members;

- Interest members in the welfare of coloured peoples in all parts of the world;

- Improve relations between the races;

- Co-operate and affiliate with organisations sympathetic to coloured people.

In 1937 the LCP added a fifth aim for the organisation which was to "render such financial assistance to coloured people in distress as lies within its capacity."

Organising the disparate and still relatively few Black people in Britain required the form of communication most commonly utilised in those far away pre-internet days – a newspaper.

The LCP published a quarterly newspaper called 'The Keys' which it was hoped would not only inform the

---

12. R. Ramdin, *The Making of the Black Working Class in Britain*, Gower, Aldershot, 1987, p.101.

readership of the campaigns and initiatives that the organisation was involved in but that it would also help to generate much needed funds.

In July 1944 the League organised a three-day conference in London to draw up a "Charter of Coloured People" that in many ways foreshadowed the resolutions of the fifth Pan-African Conference held in Manchester the following year and much later the Labour Party Black Section "Black Agenda."

The Charter demanded that there should be full self-government for colonial peoples at the earliest possible opportunity, and insisted that: "The same economic, educational, legal and political rights shall be enjoyed by all persons, male and female, whatever their colour.

All discrimination in employment, in places of public entertainment and refreshment, or in other public places, shall be illegal and shall be punished."

LCP 1931

These demands reflected two things. Firstly, the continued frustration by the LCP of the continuing highly pervasive and widespread nature of the colour bar in Britain.

It is easy to believe that the colour bar in Britain was a phenomenon that was primarily the experience of the Windrush generation.

But this would be far from the truth. There was also no legal obstacle or remedy that could be sought for acts of racism. There was to be no legal protection against racism provided by the British state until the mid-1960s.

The second imperative for the Charter was the nearing of the end of the War.

The experience of African workers after World War I, where resentment from white workers was rife and was expressed in the events of the Red Summer of 1919 (see above), could not be repeated.

Without legal protection African workers ran the risk of experiencing a repeat of history with African people laying down their lives for peace and liberty in the War only to face the prospect of returning home to face racism at work and in their social lives.

The Charter, recognising the transnational nature of the resistance to racism that was ahead, was sent to every government of the United Nations as well as to many leaders of national organisations within those countries.

In this sense the contribution of the LCP has been greatly underplayed. The LCP captured the mood of Africans in Britain as it neared the end of its contribution to the War effort.

Why should things go back the way they were? What had the fighting with Nazi Germany been for anyway? What was certain was that given that the War was worldwide there was no way that the returning African military would see the resistance to racism as being anything other than transnational.

The Empire, and the resistance within it against racism, was in many ways, alongside the soon to emerge Civil Rights Movement in the US, going to define the course of politics for the latter half of the twentieth century.

But the resistance by African workers to the attacks of 1919 underlined the importance of self-liberation to the African community.

Without self-liberation strategies within their communities African workers would likely have been routed and to make matters worse, there was only negligible support from the white-dominated institutions of the British labour and trade union movement.

It was though not just a lesson learned from 1919. It was a lesson learned from hundreds of years of collective resistance to enslavement and colonialism.

It has always been the case that African communities have never been able to wait for a knight in shining armour to come to their rescue in the fight against racism. It is a fight that Black people, even with white support, have had to lead themselves.

There was no evidence that African workers could rely on very much support from the British trade unionists or any of the left political parties.

There appeared to be a disconnect between arguing for colonial freedoms on one hand, and facing up to the racism that was being experienced by African people at home and in the communities in which they lived.

But African socialists such as Claude McKay nevertheless continued to organise for change within and outside the trade union movement and across the socialist world.

McKay, in my view, does not get enough credit for his role in helping to re-awakening the African radical tradition of self-liberation.

McKay, a writer originally from Jamaica, journeyed from the US to England in 1919 helps to provide us with a link between African people in Britain and across the rest of the English-speaking British Empire.

McKay was a fierce advocate of African liberation through Bolshevism and played a leading role in the work of the Communist International.

In response to the uprisings of 1919 McKay wrote the sonnet, *If We Must Die*, as a means of urging people to fight back:

> *"If we must die, let it not be like hogs*
> *Hunted and penned in an inglorious spot,*
> *While round us bark the mad and hungry dogs,*
> *Making their mock at our accursed lot.*
> *If we must die, O let us nobly die,*
> *So that our precious blood may not be shed*
> *In vain; then even the monsters we defy*
> *Shall be constrained to honour us though dead!*
> *O kinsmen we must meet the common foe!*
> *Though far outnumbered let us show us brave,*
> *And for their thousand blows deal one deathblow!*
> *What though before us lies the open grave?*
> *Like men we'll face the murderous, cowardly pack,*
> *Pressed to the wall, dying, but fighting back!"*

In this sonnet McKay captured the mood of the time by his recognition of the often deadly nature of African resistance.[13]

The entrenched nature of the racism being experienced by African workers led to a further disenchantment for McKay and others in the British trade union movement.

McKay saw for himself how racist propaganda was penetrating deeply into the trade union movement.

Claude McKay

---

13. C. McKay, *Constab Ballads: Including the Poem "If We Must Die"*, Ragged Hand, Bristol, 2008.

The annual Trades Union Congress, held at the Town Hall in Portsmouth in September 1920, covered by McKay for the Dreadnought newspaper, was a case in point.

At Congress a pamphlet was circulated by the Union of Democratic Control on "The Horror of the Rhine."

This pamphlet referred to an incident that had taken place in April of that year in the Rhineland in Germany.

The Germans had violated the Treaty of Versailles by extending their control of the Rhineland by occupying a number of major cities on the east bank of the river.

Although only 25,000 of the quarter of a million French troops were not European (mainly North African), the presence of Black troops occupying part of a European nation created a storm of controversy.

The *Daily Herald* and other newspapers reported the incident in openly racist terms with language such as the "black scourge" in Europe or about the "sexual horror" being let loose by France on the Rhine.

TUC delegates were apparently all too eager to agree with the racist reporting of the incident on the Rhine.

McKay was said to be deeply shocked by the attitude of the delegates to Congress and the ease with which trade unionists fell quickly into using racist tropes.

Unfortunately, while this incident did not dim the political faith or activity of McKay it was a marker for the way that some within the labour movement in Britain were quick to accept racist stereotypes (of the African man as a sexual animal) in later years.

McKay was one of the African activists fighting hard to place the issue of racism front and centre with the white revolutionary left. In 1922 he travelled to Moscow to address the Fourth World Congress of the Comintern.

When McKay addressed the Congress he criticised the racism of the American Communist Party and the labour movement.

He warned that unless the left challenged racism and white supremacy, the ruling class would continue to play African and white workers off against each other.

McKay believed that there would be no progress for the working class without African workers at its centre.

The Communist International responded to the plea for support from McKay by forming a specific so-called Negro Commission and committing resources to recruiting more Black cadres and being more active in supporting African liberation across the world.

The Comintern, having been impressed by his speech to the Congress, also commissioned McKay to put his thoughts into a book. This was published in Russia as "The Negroes in America."

This turned out to be an important book that helped to re-shape Comintern policy.

McKay argued that any commitment to African freedom could not ignore the need to support self-organisation as well as self-determination on the road to African liberation.

He also used the book to call on the left to provide more support than it had been doing to the newly emerging African-nationalist movements.

Pioneering African socialists, such as McKay, were also involved in political activity in their countries of origin.

They were part of an historic period of African radical awakening against colonialism and racism.

Whilst African self-liberation strategies are sometimes characterised as separatist this seems to ignore the agency of the oppressed to decide and act on their own means of liberation.

The resistance to racism within Britain was (and is) as we have seen with the seafarers, particularly acute within the workplace.

The workplace, after all, represents the front line in the continuing struggle between capital and labour and, consequently, the necessary resistance to the racism generated by capital.

It should then come as little surprise that during this period the first independent African self-organised trade union in Britain was formed. After all, the numbers of African workers in the workforce increased during the inter-war years, particularly in key ports such as Cardiff, Liverpool, and in the capital city of London.

But there were also significant numbers of African workers in sectors outside of the ports.

The Coloured Film Artistes' Association

The TUC archives show that the Coloured Film Artistes' Association (CFAA) was established at Elstree studios during the late 1930s. It was a means of attempting to improve the terms and conditions of work for Black actors and extras at the site.

The CFAA sought affiliation to the TUC in 1939 but

their application was unsuccessful in part due to the attitude of the National Association of Theatrical and Kine Employees (NATKE).

NATKE Badge

NATKE, on the surface, opposed the application by the CFAA on the grounds that unions already existed for actors and extras.

But, the TUC files on this application reveal what were covert racist comments over the difficulty of determining the demarcation line between the CFAA and another union, the Oriental Film Artistes' Union that had also applied for affiliation to the TUC.

This is an important and, yet again, another under-researched milestone in the development of African self-liberation.

Having recognised the central role played by trade unions in the entertainment industry in working with employers to regulate access to the labour market, these groups of workers challenged what they clearly regarded as the racially based nature of that regulation.

They decided to self-organise as workers and to seek the same right to representation and access to that particular part of the labour market on the same basis enjoyed by white workers. Unfortunately, as we see above, their effort to join the "union club" was doomed to failure.

The union was effectively "blackballed" by the trade union movement.

The ultimate end of the union should not disguise the importance of this initiative for the later development of African self-liberation strategies in British trade unions.

The Windrush Legacy

This section traces the key influences on the development of African self-liberation from after World War II through to the beginning of the British Civil Rights and Black Power movements.

This era, commonly known as the Windrush era, after the ship that arrived in the UK in 1948 from the Caribbean, is often used to symbolise the start of post-war immigration to Britain.

Windrush ship

In reality it heralded the start of post-war Black migration to Britain. White immigration was already a long-standing fact of life that was hardly worth a blip of concern on the radar of most commentators.

A simple line drawn after 1945 would mean yet another failure to appreciate the momentous impact that the war itself had on the development of Black worker consciousness, organisation and resistance.

A system of racism, in its own way, at times every bit as rigid and hurtful as anything that existed under the Jim Crow system in the US, had already developed in Britain to keep Black workers in their place.

There were three recognisable by-products of the colour bar in Britain.

Firstly, there was the encouragement that it gave to racists within and outside of the workplace.

Secondly, there was the re-emergence of the phenomenon that we witnessed during the Red Summer of 1919, that of blaming the victims of racism for the attacks being made on them – clearly, according to the racist conception, if Black workers were not in Britain then there would be no trouble!

This, as in 1919, leads to the third by-product of the colour bar – that of a call for stronger immigration controls.

The difference in the Windrush era was that the call for stronger immigration controls was fully joined by the trade union movement.

But rather than being a story of victims it is actually a tale of how the principles and benefits of Black collective resistance to racism, forged in the Caribbean Islands under enslavement and colonialism, was adapted for use in the new environment of Britain.

It was this Black collectivism that was to lead to strong expressions of wider Black political activity and, alongside it, African self-liberation strategies in British trade unions.

Black resistance to racism in Britain during the post-war years cannot be seen in isolation from all of the experiences that Black workers faced and endured in previous times.

This is a central point to this book. This was no less the case with the impact that the experiences of being African during the war years had in helping to shape future resistance to racism.

One could almost forgive a reader of World War II history for thinking that all of the racism that went before the war was forgotten or put to one side for the common and overriding goal of defeating the Nazis and their allies.

This was, unfortunately, not the case.

Racism was as acute during the war as it ever was. Indeed, it was arguably precisely because the British and their allies saw the war effort as more important than anything that African workers found themselves confronted by a new phase of racism in Britain as well as in the colonies.

The arrival of ships such as the SS Windrush (which docked on June 22nd 1948 with its 492 West Indian passengers) was still a rarity. Immigration of West Indians to Britain during this early period was very small and far from organised.

Ships to Britain from the Caribbean Islands were not regular and it was only when demand grew for cheap labour that the business of migration really took off.

Of course the business of migration (because that is what it was for a small elite who sold the tickets and owned the means of transport) to Britain did not just occur because of the demands for cheap labour in the "Mother Country".

Windrush passengers

One of the other main reasons for the migration of African workers from the West Indies to Britain after World War II was the high levels of unemployment in the colonies, and, if you did manage to find work, low wages allied to poor opportunities for progress.

In Britain there was at least the promise of or hope for something better for West Indians – a brighter future for them and for their children.

Even though Britain was tied to the English-speaking Caribbean through its colonial conquests it was never a foregone conclusion that it would be the first option for migration.

The US casts a heavy shadow over the Caribbean and, after all, the mythology of the possible riches on offer in the States was arguably more seductive than that on offer in Britain.

However, the McCarran-Walter Act of 1952 did much to remove the option of West Indian migration to the USA while some took the option of moving to Canada.

With access to the US restricted and the legal right of entry into Britain already guaranteed, the choice of where to go to seek an improvement in one's economic and social situation was a simple one.

Indeed, the choice was made even easier by the explicit invitation made by the British Government for African workers from the West Indies to come and help to rebuild their post-war economy.

In reality the invitation from the British government was to help fill a post-war labour shortage – for African workers to do the jobs that white workers no longer wished to do, and, for cheaper.

This period of migration must be seen within a proper context.

Workers from other parts of the world were also migrating to Britain after World War II. The fact was that white immigration was not a concern. White immigrants could easily become lost in the indigenous population, over a relatively short period of time orally but, visually, immediately.

No such possibility existed for Black workers. Key to defining whether or not you were classed as a migrant or (the more negative connotation) an immigrant was colour rather than language, culture or customs.

On that basis, African workers could easily be identified and, therefore, singled out for "special" treatment.

The year 1948 was also notable for the reaction of the white leadership of the British trade union movement.

The *Liverpool Echo*, during 1948, reported a speech from the annual conference of the National Union of Seamen, where it was made very clear that Black workers were not wanted on the ports of Britain. The delegate said:

> "In quite a few instances we have been successful in changing ships from coloured to white, and in many instances in persuading masters and engineers that white men should be carried in preference to coloured."

The *Echo* went on to report that "committees have been set up in the main ports to vet all coloured entrants to the country who claim to be seamen."

The NUS was merely a barometer for some of the negative attitudes that existed in the trade union movement in Britain towards African workers.

These attitudes did not only stimulate workplace divisions but it also was part of the general trend that led towards violence against the African community in the very year of the arrival of the Windrush.

Liverpool, so often portrayed, on the one hand, as the bell-weather for race relations in Britain, and, on the other, as a bastion of socialist politics, was the scene of violent attacks against the Black community.

Foreshadowing what was to take place during the early 1980s, the African community of Liverpool was the victim of Police racism.

This time, rather than the routine harassment that was to become the norm in the 1970s and 80s, the police mobilised against the African community who were defending themselves against violent attacks during the early days of August 1948.

A 300 strong white mob attacked an African man coming out of an Indian restaurant before trashing the premises.

The next day, around 2,000 whites attacked a hostel for Black seamen.

When Africans decided to barricade themselves in against attack from local whites at a club on the third night, the police, instead of prioritising upholding the law, decided to storm the building and confront those inside as whites outside looked on.

An investigation by authorities into the attack against the Africans in the club brought about two significant outcomes.

Firstly, it helped to create a level of solidarity between all parts of the African community in Liverpool.

Secondly, it confirmed to the African community, in Liverpool and across the rest of the country, that they could not necessarily expect support from elsewhere, including the local trade union and labour movement, when under attack.

Far from being surprised by the attacks against them, the African community was only too well aware of what racism meant and the dangers that faced them.

The only alternative, one learned in the immediate past under British colonial rule and, before that, under slavery and indentured labour, was, as always, to rely on each other to find the best ways of forging an effective resistance to racism.

Darcus Howe, the writer and broadcaster, writing in the *New Statesman* on the fiftieth anniversary of the arrival of the Windrush, provides a view of the relationship with the trade union movement during this period:

Howe said: "We were compulsorily unionised but the ambivalence of our representatives created some tension: on the one hand, we were part of the working class, on the other, we were foreigners taking the jobs of locals and undermining wage rates.

He added that the phrase "'Workers of the world unite' was a slogan conveniently discarded by union and party alike".[14]

Later, in the same article Howe goes on to assert the class consciousness of the new arrivals and how, because of the trade unions born from the insurrections in the Caribbean islands, the newcomers had taken "to British unions and the Labour Party as ducks to the pond".[15]

One might add to Howe's second comments that any class consciousness held by the newcomers was in spite of the attitudes and actions of some in trade unions and the Labour Party.

---

14. D. Howe, *New Statesman*, 12 July 1998, p.30.
15. Ibid.

The Colour Bar

The "special" treatment that African workers were subjected to in Britain from white workers was often very direct and extremely degrading.

From the beginning of this new period of migration, because, as I have mentioned elsewhere, this was not a new phenomenon, African workers were segregated in much the same way that we have since come to understand the Jim Crow system of racism that took place in the Southern States of America.

The type of work that the new workers in Britain were recruited to do was typically at the very bottom of the labour market.

The recruitment to different sectors of the economy also depended on where in the world you were from.

Pakistani and Bangladeshi workers were specifically recruited by employer agents to work in the textile industries while Indian workers were employed predominantly in foundries and low-skilled manufacturing roles.

Caribbean workers of African descent were substantially recruited to work in the then nationalised railway industry and other areas of public transport in jobs that white workers did not want to do.

The division of Black labour into African and Asian created immense difficulties for the development of unity of action against the racial discrimination that all Black groups regardless of national heritage faced. It also provided a precursor for the later difficulties posed by so-called diversity management.

This was however not a hindrance to the recognition by Black workers that self-liberation strategies to resist racism were necessary. It just meant that the unity between Black activists was patchy and more difficult to organise and maintain.

The instant communication systems, such as computers and mobile phones simply did not exist for the Windrush generation. Access to personal home telephones was not as widespread as it is now and neither was ready access to anything other than public transport.

Travelling away from the comfort of an area where others from your own community lived often placed one in peril of attack from racists. The reality was that it was just plain difficult to be in the same place at the same time to organise.

One example of what could happen in Britain when Black workers were in an environment to organise was the formation of the first, and to date only, independent Black self-organised trade union in the country, the Coloured Film Artistes' Association (see above).

However, there were examples of other more localised and innovative attempts by Black workers to overcome the problem of logistics to self-organise in the workplace.

Sivanandan (1986) tells us of the skilled African workers who met secretly during 1951.

He tells of how these workers met "in lavatories and wash rooms to form a West Indian association which could take up cases of discrimination.

"But the employers soon found out and they were driven to hold their meetings in a neighbouring barber's shop – from which point the association became more community oriented".[16]

While this group and others like it were really more like social and welfare organisations, they did still seek to tackle the racism that was being experienced by Black workers, African or Asian, in the workplace.

In fact, rather than the importance of these formations being reduced they were vital survival and resistance mechanisms for the workers. They were also an important forerunner of the informal methods of Black self-liberation strategies that we still see today.

These informal formations were vital for a unified Black resistance to racism. This was particularly the case because the assistance forthcoming from trade unions to resist workplace and community racism was, at best, marginal. It also showed the ingenuity that Black workers were forced to use in organising communities of resistance to racism.

It is no coincidence that these initiatives bear a striking similarity to the strategies that were used to resist racism "back home" under colonial rule or, much earlier, under slavery.

The lesson, well-learnt, was that African resistance did not require a formal committee room, minutes of meetings or strict rules and procedures. In fact, writing anything down under strict colonial rule could have seriously damaged your health – or even cost you your life.

The lesson was that you met, agreed what needed to be done, went away and did what was agreed, and then came back and told everyone that you had carried out your task.

16. Sivanandan, 'From Resistance to Rebellion', p. 113.

A logical extension of the great oral traditions of Africa that also gave you an opportunity for survival during both enslavement and colonialism.

Forging the unity necessary to resist racism, firstly between African workers, then African and Asian workers as well as Black and white workers in Britain had two important drivers.

One was the "colour-bar" and the other was institutional racism arising from State immigration controls.

The colour-bar, or Black exclusion from public and private housing, social clubs and public houses as well as from some banking facilities, was also widespread in British workplaces.

The workplace colour-bar, which was particularly acute in the immediate aftermath of World War II, usually took the form of Black workers being excluded from the sorts of jobs that earned enhanced bonus payments or were restricted to particular low paid or graded levels of work that held little prospects for promotion.

Black workers in Britain are still experiencing the legacy of this form of racism today.

TUC reports regularly reveal how Black workers still experience doing the same work as white workers for less pay.[17]

The application of the colour-bar drew no distinction between those of African, African-Caribbean or Asian descent.

From the thugs on the street, attacking often defenceless Black people, to the pub landlord denying a Black

---

17. TUC, 2004.

person the chance to buy a drink there was none of the niceties – for the racists they were all Black.

The British government did little to oppose these acts of discrimination. Indeed the government itself was guilty of enacting legislation that was deliberately designed to exclude immigrants from particular commonwealth countries.

The Commonwealth Immigrants Act of 1962 effectively nationalised racism.

The Act was clear that if labour from the "darker nations" (as Vijay Prashad termed it) was still required then its use was going to be heavily regulated by the state.

This legislation set the standard for future immigration controls. More immigration restrictions on entry were applied in 1965 and 1971.

The 1971 Immigration Act in particular did not just seek to provide a degree of regulation, it was designed to all but halt immigration to Britain from all but the white colonies such as Canada and Australia or the US.

The only Black people now permitted to enter were white or, if you were African or Asian, under the terms of a contract labour system that was for a specified period and to carry out designated tasks.

The policy of the British state – that essentially said African or Asian (as distinct from other forms of) immigration was a problem – was the green light for racism – if in fact such encouragement was needed.

The Black community, feeling the brunt of the unleashed racism that preceded and followed the 1962 Immigration Act were compelled to organise to resist the attacks that were being made against them.

Organisations such as the Pakistani Workers' Association
and the West Indian Workers' Association (both founded
in 1961) were prominent self-organised groups that were
active in the resistance to racism in Britain at that time.

After all it was through such communities of resistance
that Black workers had always responded to attacks
made against them.

immigration Act protests

One might reasonably ask about the trade union movement attitude in the great immigration debate, particularly given its impact on Black workers as well as on employment relations more generally.

Illustrative of the trade union position is the attitude of the National Union of Railwaymen (NUR) which, in 1957 contacted the TUC "to declare its support for some form of immigration control".[18]

The nationalised railway industry was one of the largest beneficiaries of the new Black migration. The role of these Black workers was largely to carry out the jobs that white workers did not want to do.

In the closed-shop workplaces of the time this meant more members and therefore more income for the NUR. But this appears to have been secondary to pandering to the racism of some white workers to the arrival of Black colleagues in their industry.

The TUC *General Council Report* to its Congress of 1958, no doubt encouraged by the attitude of influential unions such as the NUR, expressed its concern over the lack of immigration controls from the Commonwealth. The report said:

> "It was suggested to the Minister of Labour that controls adopted by other self-governing Commonwealth countries should be studied and that it would be suitable for Britain to adopt some measures of control over would-be immigrants for whom no job is waiting or is likely to be available.

18. Ramdin, *The Making of the Black Working Class in Britain*

It was also suggested that a medical
examination should be included within these
immigration controls".[19]

We see here that the TUC not only supported the
notion that entry to Britain should be determined by the
availability of jobs but that they also believed that health
levels were a determining factor.

These are themes that recur time and again during
debates in later years around immigration. The common
factor appears to be the desire to apply these conditions
only to "black countries".

Immigration in Britain was and still is a euphemism for
race. The debate was not concerned with immigration
from "white" nations – this was simply not a factor in
the debate.

The concern was to deal with immigration from Black
Commonwealth countries. This appears to have been
as much of a concern for the TUC at the time as it was
(and still is) for the wider public policy debate.

The reality was that during this period the TUC
nationally was simply no help in resisting the racism
being experienced by the growing Black community.
Indeed, the TUC at the time was for much tighter
(Black) immigration controls.

The TUC *General Council Report* (1967) expressed
reservations about a government proposal to put
clauses in government contracts that would forbid
discrimination – what has now become known as
contract compliance. The TUC said:

---

19. Trades Union Congress, *Report of the Proceedings of the 90th Annual TUC*, 1958, p.378.

"Work people who were to be protected from discrimination might be put in a privileged position, since there was no limitation on the right to engage or dismiss others without reasons being given."[20]

My reason for touching on TUC immigration and race relations policy is to underline that for Black workers support from the officialdom of the trade union movement against the racism they were experiencing, whether at work or elsewhere, could not be guaranteed. In fact the opposite in most cases appeared to be the case.

It was therefore inevitable that African workers looked to themselves, as they had always done throughout history, to find the best methods of resisting racism.

In short, there was little alternative than to fall back on the need to form Black communities of resistance.

Although at a national level there was little or no support in resisting racism there were certainly honourable examples of more local attempts to support Black workers.

Nottingham Trades Council, for example, set up a liaison committee with Black immigrants as far back as 1954.

The trades council even paid for the cost of a booklet that welcomed Black immigrants to the City and, while strongly criticising one of the largest local unions for discriminatory policies (causing the union to withdraw from the trades council), encouraged African and Asian workers to join trade unions.

It was clear to Black workers, as it seemed apparent to Nottingham Trades Council, that racism in the workplace was prevalent and therefore resistance was not only necessary, but vital.

20. Trades Union Congress, *General Council Report*, 1967, p.236.

Public transport sector, particularly on the buses, was
perhaps the area of employment that white resistance to
African employment received most publicity.

Wright says that: "According to press reports,
bus company employees in several towns (e.g.
Bristol, Coventry, West Bromwich, Birmingham,
Wolverhampton, Nottingham and Newcastle-upon-
Tyne) and also railway workers in Birmingham
and London have at various times objected to the
employment of coloured (sic) workers".[21]

The West Indian Standing Conference, an organisation
formed in the aftermath of serious so called 'race riots'
in Nottingham and in Notting Hill, West London during
September 1958 (see Ramdin, 1987 pp 204-216 for a
detailed account of these disturbances) also published
literature on the colour bar in transport (July, 1967).

Not only were African workers forced to tackle the
racism of white employers but they also had to face
up to the fact that trade unions, that were more than
happy to accept their membership subscriptions, were
not always willing to stand up for them against the daily
grind of racism in the workplace and beyond.

Indeed, on many occasions, unions were entirely
complicit in the racism experienced by African workers.

This in many ways made it inevitable that the African
radical tradition of forming communities of resistance to
racism would be called upon in the latest battle against
racism in Britain.

21. PL Wright, *The Coloured Worker in British Industry*, Institute of Race Relations/Oxford
University Press, London, 1968 pp 61-62.

African self-liberation strategies arrived in Britain on the wave of the anti-colonial struggles in the Caribbean and Africa, as well as South Asia.

Black self-organised union structures in Britain were used by African and Asian workers as a community of resistance to defeat the ideological objections from white (as well as some Black) trade unionists to self-liberation.

These developments, in the long run, helped to build stronger alliances between progressive Black and white anti-racists and deepened the anti-racist agenda within unions and "progressive" political parties.

The Long 1970s

Whilst, as I have shown, informal and more formal African self-liberation groups have existed in and outside the workplace for most of the twentieth century, they began to substantially emerge as a force within British trade unions during the 1970s and some of these achieved formal status during the 1980s.

The roots of what was now a multi-layered Black liberation struggle in Britain in the 1970s, of which the trade unions were one arena, began in the 1960s – creating a long decade.

Much of the resistance to racism that showed appeared as communities of resistance followed on from the Black political activity generated by the activities of Enoch Powell and his infamous "Rivers of Blood" speech in 1968 as well as the civil rights and Black power movements of the tumultuous 1960s.

It is perhaps a little too seductive (not to say simplistic) to overstate the air of radicalism that is so readily used to characterise the 1960s – particularly the latter stages of that decade.

For the vast majority of the African community in Britain the economic situation was dire and so the 1960s were just another time to struggle against racism.

The 60s brought with it a greater sense of political awareness for most Africans in Britain and across the diaspora.

The challenge of the 1960s was essentially the same as it had always been – survival and resistance – at whatever level and by whatever means possible.

The ambition of the Windrush generation to create better opportunities for their children was in full flow during the 1960s.

The second generation (as we became known) were making our way through the school system and all the racism that that entailed at the time.

So for most African people in Britain whether in the workplace or simply trying to get an education, resisting racism, one way or another, was a matter of everyday life and not optional.

It was this experience of racism that helped to frame the lives of those that entered the workplaces of the 1970s in the knowledge that there were likely to be few others who would be likely to stand alongside them.

Doing it themselves, through communities of resistance, wasn't just something to think about doing for African political and trade union activists, it was, for many, realistically, the only show in town.

The roots of African resistance to racism in Britain owed a debt far wider than the experience garnered on these shores. It was, as I have shown, a continued expression of the experience of anti-colonial resistance and the prior struggles of the Pan-Africanist movements.

There were no blank slates arriving in Britain during the Windrush years.

Everyone arriving in Britain after World War II had an experience of life.

These lives were often hard and shaped by the harsh realities of British colonial rule. Many individuals arrived with a clear understanding of political and trade union organising and the bitter experience of the realities of racism.

This left the stark choice between acceptance or resistance.

The African experience in Britain was a particularly British one. It was different, as I will show, from the US African experience even though it shared a number of similarities.

The liberation struggles of Africans in 1970s Britain was a much more militant expression of the radical tradition than had previously been seen in Britain.

Local African political organisations, such as the Black Unity and Freedom Party, the Black Workers Co-ordinating Committee and the Croydon Collective began to emerge during this time (see below).

These organisations were the training ground for African activists who went on to become active in unions and in campaigns for greater African representation.

Demands grew for trade unions to take more action against racism in the workplace and over issues such as police harassment.

However, there was no real national focus to this work – a vacuum that the trade union movement should have, but did not fill.

It was to be some years after World War II before the trade union movement was to be seen as much more of a partner in wider anti-racist and anti-fascist mobilisations.

Activists from organisations such the Black Unity and Freedom Party, and a wide range of other small formations, went on to become active in other larger Black self-organised groups such as the Black Trade Unionists Solidarity Movement (BTUSM) – set up in December 1981.

The founders of BTUSM were concerned about the extent of racism in British society and in particular in the trades unions and labour movement.[22]

Although it was established in 1981 the first conference of BTUSM was held at County Hall, London on 4-5 June 1983. This should be recognised as a decisive step by trade unionists of African and Asian descent in Britain.

These Black workers were no longer prepared to accept being largely ignored by the trade union movement and their often oblivious attitude towards racism. BTUSM made it clear that its approach was for change within and not without the trade union movement.

Ramdin (1987) highlights this as a particularly important feature of the BTUSM development:

---

22. Black Trade Unionists Solidarity Movement, *Declaration*, Issue No.1., 1981.

"........they have clearly stated their intention to organise and work within the trade union movement. In other words, they want white workers to recognise and act on the real, day-to day problems of racism and sexism so that together they can work effectively".[23]

The demands made by the BTUSM also required party political support.

To achieve this political change, particular emphasis needed to be placed on influencing the Labour Party – the political party that had managed to secure the loyalty of the vast majority of Black voters without ever really having done much to deal with racism.

Many of the same BTUSM activists helped to found the Labour Party Black Sections movement, even though a number could never actually bring themselves to become members of such a reactionary Party.

The campaign to secure official recognition for the Black Sections community of resistance within the Labour Party is instructive for how a coalescence of trade union and mainstream political activity began to take place for a number of Black activists.

It is arguable that the Black Sections' cause began to gain more traction when Black self-liberation groups began to be won within trade unions.

But it was the self-liberation fights within the trade union movement that was to have the deepest and ongoing influence.

The movement for Black self-liberation groups within

---

23 Ramdin, *The Making of the Black Working Class in Britain*, pp.368-9.

the Labour Party arose from the struggles and the deepest frustrations with the Labour Movement during the 1970s.

Time and time again the leadership of the Labour Movement was being shown to be taking Black workers for granted both in terms of their vote and in their membership of unions.

Nowhere was this frustration more clearly displayed than at the historic Imperial Typewriters dispute in 1974. This is one of the most important struggles by Black workers in British history.

The Imperial Typewriters Strike of 1974 is often cited by trade unionists as a historic example of how the trade union movement rallied together to support a group of predominantly Asian workers in a workplace struggle.

Strikes, or any other form of industrial action, do not just occur. A range of circumstances come together to force workers to take the ultimate and always difficult step of withdrawing their labour.

Imperial Typewriters strike 1974

The strike at Imperial owed much to the influence
that the British Empire still exercises on popular
consciousness.

Many of the white supremacist notions still held today
about Black inferiority were demonstrated at Imperial.

Sivanandan referred to the strike as the "apotheosis of
racism….and therefore the resistance to it."[24]

The strike at Imperial began, rather appropriately,
on International Workers Day, May 1, 1974, when 39
workers walked out from the plant.

Within a week the strikers at Imperial were followed
by 500 others who walked out in support. The Asian
workers went on strike in protest against their low pay
– men averaged around £25 a week and women £18 –
and the operation of the bonus scheme.

The focus of this book is around African rather than
Asian workers but there are just a couple of points I
want to draw from this important strike around the role
of building communities of resistance after a strike that
was ultimately lost and saw the plant close down.

Firstly, one of the key demands by the strikers was
around representation. They wanted the right to elect
their own shop stewards as members of the then
Transport and General Workers Union (TGWU).

For the 1600 workers on the site (of which
approximately 1100 were Asian) there were 16 shop
stewards who were all appointed – not elected – by the
TGWU factory convenor Reg Weaver.

24. A. Sivanandan, *A Different Hunger: Writings on Black Resistance*, Pluto Press, London, 1982.

Second was the way the workers' grievances about racist treatment in the payment of wages was dealt with by the union.

George Bromley, the local full-time TGWU official, criticised the workers, accusing them of failing to follow a proper disputes procedure and that "some people must learn how things are done."[25]

Management and union officials sided in refusing to negotiate with what they regarded as Asian "troublemakers" and "outside agitators", the chief amongst these being a South African of Asian origin called Bennie Bunsee, who was acting as an advisor to the strikers.

Bunsee had been an advisor to Asian workers during various industrial disputes, such as Mansfield Hosiery.

In later years Bunsee, a Pan-Africanist Congress of Azania activist in exile from South Africa during the apartheid years, was a leading activist in the Labour Party Black Sections struggles of the 1980s.

He was never a Labour Party member but played an important advisory role for the Black Sections activists as a staunch advocate of the principles of Black self-organisation within the labour movement.

But it is the third point that is instructive about how communities of resistance against racism refused to be tied down to the boundaries of a workplace.

The workers turned to their community for help, in the same way that other Asian strikers had sought and received help at other disputes such as Perivale

---

25. F. Dhondy, 'The Strike at Imperial Typewriters' in *Race Today*, July 1974.

Gutermann, Harwood Cash Lawn Mills in Mansfield, Malmic Lace in Nottingham (all during 1973) and Mansfield Hosiery Mills a year earlier in 1972.

The strikers turned to their communities not only because of a lack of union support but also because self-liberation was one of their most immediate experiences.

Making arrangements for their own social facilities, informal saving arrangements as well as co-operation and support on housing, was a common experience.

This self-liberation extended to what Sivanandan describes as the standing conference of Black strike committees. These networks extended across the

Bennie Bunse

Midlands area during that time alongside a patchwork of Black political organisations that were ready to come to the aid of the workers.

Imperial Typewriters was but the latest in a series of important episodes of Black resistance to racism.

At the end of May 1974 most of the strikers were sacked by Imperial and never did secure official union support or recognition for their dispute.

The strike at Imperial was arguably the most important example of a wave of Black resistance to racism by Black workers in the industrial arena.

It was notable that these Black workers had no recourse but to rely on each other, from within their own community, to organise against racism, in the absence of official union support.

This was Black self-liberation at its rawest – born from necessity in the face of the refusal of the trade union movement to provide the recognition and support that could have been reasonably expected in an industrial dispute by workers over terms and conditions albeit with the added ingredient of racism.

The long tradition of Black self-liberation, rooted in a legacy of resistance to slavery, indentured labour and colonialism as well as to the racist hostility faced by many workers of African and Asian origin in the workplace was crystallised at Imperial.

Self-liberation communities of resistance, of which the strike at Imperial was a practical expression, was a strategy that would later, as I show below, inform the growth of Black political groups and organisations within and outside trade unions through the remainder of the 1970s and into the 1980s and 90s.

In this respect the strike at Imperial Typewriters should be seen as central to the development of Black self-liberation within the British labour movement.

The importance of the strategy of developing and maintaining unity between people of African and Asian descent was brought front and centre once Margaret Thatcher was elected as leader of the Conservative Party in 1975 and proceeded, once elected as prime minister in 1979, to further embed the institutionalisation of racism in British society and, in the process, deepen the divisions between Black and white workers.

Thatcherism
– The Institutionalisation of Racism

During a television interview in January 1978, just 10 years after the Powell Rivers of Blood speech, Margaret Thatcher said "people are really rather afraid that this country might be rather swamped by people with a different culture."

She added, there was a fear that British people (for which she meant white) felt they "might be swamped"[26] by people coming into the country – for which she meant Black people.

Thatcher also made it clear that a new Tory government would all but end Black immigration.

After defeating the Labour Party at the 1979 General Election Thatcher set about using the African and Asian communities as the scapegoats for the economic

---

26. M. Thatcher, *Granada Television interview*, 27 January 1978.

crisis that the country was in and which she was about to worsen by her wilful destruction of the country's industrial base.

The 1980 Nationality Bill was the first shot in this new onslaught.

The Bill would also serve to steal the political ground that was once occupied by the far-right National Front by scapegoating the Black community, once again, as being the problem rather than the racism that they were experiencing.

The subsequent 1981 British Nationality Act thoroughly redefined who was and, perhaps more importantly, who was not a British citizen.

The Act removed the right to British nationality simply on the basis of birth within the Empire.

Margaret Thatcher

So while on the one hand lamenting the demise of the Empire and wrapping herself in the flag, on the other hand Thatcher removed one of the central foundations that it had boasted – that everyone within the Empire was under the protection of the Crown because they were British.

The exception to this new rule was where at least one parent was either a British national or "settled" in Britain, you theoretically had unlimited leave to remain.

The White Paper published prior to the British Nationality Bill was revealing for its candour.

The White Paper said: "The Government's main uneasiness on this score is that allowing birth to confer citizenship on a child (of parents neither of whom is a British Citizen and neither of whom is free of conditions of stay) means also that after he returns with his parents to their country, his own children, born years later, will be British citizens by descent.

> "The additional British Citizen so created, with the right of abode here, would form a pool of considerable size, and they would have little or no real connection with the United Kingdom."[27]

The resulting legislation severely limited the right of nationality based on birth in Britain to children of whom at least one parent is either a British national or settled, and gave a limited nationality to persons born abroad to those of whom one parent was born (or registered, naturalised or adopted).

The race-based nature of immigration and nationality policies was clarified for anyone that needed clarification.

27. British Government, *White Paper*, Command no 7987, July 1980, paragraph 43, p.8.

The Thatcher era served to further entrench the institutional racism that owed its roots to the 1961 Immigration Act in recent times and the legislation to restrict Black seafarers in the early part of the twentieth century.

As before the racism now being experienced by Africans and Asians was enforced ruthlessly by the police through the targeted use of stop and search and harassment.

Thatcher gave a green light to racism that many felt able to drive though.

The Black community could not even find a space for relaxation at events such as professional football matches. The football grounds became virtual no-go zones for many in the Black community because of the level of racism directed towards the few African players that were plying their trade in the professional game.

The terraces were breeding grounds for fascist organisations such as the National Front who then took their hatred into local communities.

The toxic brew of high levels of unemployment and harassment, including from the police, was a powder keg waiting to explode.

It was inevitable that Black people, both African and Asian, would eventually take steps to resist the racism that they were experiencing.

The powder keg exploded with street uprisings in the inner-city areas of St. Paul's in Bristol, during April 1980, followed by Brixton in South London (April 1981) and, later Toxteth in Liverpool as well as Southall in West London.

Lord Scarman was appointed by the Thatcher Government to lead an inquiry into the riots in Brixton.

Brixton was particularly significant as it was widely held to be the spiritual home of the African community – earning the label "The front line."

The Inquiry was charged with examining both the immediate and underlying causes of what the Government called "disturbances" and many in the Black community termed an 'uprising'.

In his findings Scarman said poor housing and lack of employment opportunities were key reasons for the uprisings but he also condemned the racist behaviour of some police officers while falling short of labelling the whole of the Metropolitan Police as racists.

Scarman's recommendations included the appointment of more Black police officers, improved police training, an independent element in the police complaints procedure and a review of the use of stop and search laws.

None of this tackled the fundamental problem of the permission being given by the police and other authorities to act in a racist manner.

The lesson for the Black community was one that it had come across before – that there are no knights in shining armour waiting to come to our rescue. Self-liberation was the only way forward.

St Pauls Riot

The Trade Union Movement and racism during the 1970s and 80s

The trade union movement during the latter part of the 1970s, particularly after the passing of the 1976 Race Relations Act, began, almost imperceptibly, to move from what could generously be called its colour-blind approach and, less generously, its indifference to the plight of Black workers, towards a more widespread recognition of the need to tackle racism.

As Ramdin accurately points out, the TUC General Council had:

"....placed less emphasis upon dealing with the material disadvantage of Black workers. Instead, it followed a two-pronged policy: first, to press all affiliated unions to negotiate acceptance by employers of equal opportunity clauses and, secondly, to press both government and the CBI to pursue equal opportunity policies."[28]

The position of the TUC, and certainly the major unions, has remained largely unchanged since that time even with some of the initiatives arising from the various anti-racism task forces they established.

While in itself the policy represented a significant shift for the TUC from one that Black workers and white anti-racists might, at best, call ambivalent, and, at worst, racist, to one that recognised that racism was an issue that needed to be more consistently faced up too.

The problem with this approach for Black workers and

28. Ramdin, *The Making of the Black Working Class in Britain*, p.361.

white anti-racists was that there were seemingly too few concrete results that could be pointed too.

Black workers, particularly those of African descent, were still facing high levels of racism in the workplace – presuming they could get employment.

There were also too many examples of white union representatives failing to provide basic representation to deal with the problems Black workers felt that they were experiencing at work.

It was increasingly clear to anyone that cared to look that the ability of the TUC to force unions to do anything that they felt unable or unwilling to do on equality issues was virtually non-existent.

Most unions did nothing to challenge the racist employment and recruitment practices of employers and rarely employed or elected African or Asian full-time officials who had direct experience of the issues.

Worse still, many trade union members were still the perpetrators of racism in the workplace and, rather than standing up to these members, trade union stewards and officials far too often failed to tackle the problem. Instead, excuses for inaction by union officials were far too frequent.

One of the earliest signs that the TUC and its affiliates were beginning to more fully engage with Black workers to challenge racism in the UK were the publication of the TUC *Charter Against Racism* followed by the first TUC *Workbook on Tackling Racism* in 1989.

These publications marked the beginning of the end of the overt culture of trade union bureaucracies believing that they understood the racism out of some magical reaction that took place when they became an official or carried a Labour or left-wing party membership card.

But for all the difficulties still ahead, at least the trade union movement had finally arrived at the party.

The tackling racism workbook was primarily a resource for TUC education courses. This underlined the common-held view that more specific education of union representatives around the issues of racism was necessary.

While it is hard to argue against this – and I certainly would not want to – this approach was firmly within the newly emerging tradition of "celebrating/managing diversity" approach with a largely skills-based "apolitical" approach to challenging racism.

Tackling the deep-seated power relationships that lay at the heart of racism, and which were so entrenched within the labour and trade union movement, was very much harder to persuade unions to do.

However, the first TUC workbook was an important milestone in terms of TUC strategies for challenging racism. It also raised the prospect for Black workers that trade unions were at last on the road to taking more seriously the issues of which they had complained of for many years.

The first workbook on racism was important because it provided the first real "official" focal point for discussions about the nature of racism and the trade union role in tackling it.

Trade unions were able to run their own tackling racism courses, using the workbook as a key resource. Unions were also able to take advantage of the tackling racism programme for their officials provided by an excellent team of tutors based at the TUC National Education Centre in Hornsey, North London.

The TUC eventually closed the centre, the former Hornsey College of Art, in 2004.

A number of other resources were produced by the TUC to support the education process. *The Guide to Tackling Race Discrimination at Work* was published by the TUC in 1995 to teach union representatives and full-time officials how to use the Race Relations Act 1976. The emphasis here was to develop the technical approach to tackling racism – typical of the TUC approach at this time.

By the time of the second *Tackling Racism Workbook* in 2001 the circumstances as well as the architecture of the TUC campaign against racism had changed markedly. By that time the TUC was responding in a more coherent way to both institutional racism and the increased appeal of the political far right.

For Black workers the period of time between the first and second workbooks was a time period when Black communities of resistance spread across the trade union movement. The structures within the TUC were also forced to change to meet the challenges.

However during the 1980s the developing struggle for Black workers was that while all these developments were taking place, there were few Black workers involved at influential levels.

There were virtually no senior Black union full time or lay officials in the movement during the 1980s and 90s.

Fred McKenzie, who was the first Black general secretary of a TUC union – leading the union that made musical instruments for the military, and Bill Morris, who later became the general secretary of the TGWU, were the only two prominent leading Black trade unionists.

But it would be a mistake to reduce this discussion to being about the numbers of African or Asian trade unionists in senior positions.

One look at the current Tory government front bench shows that this is a road to nowhere.

Understanding the importance of class interests and racism - "super exploitation" - is the key.

As discontent by Black workers with the trade union movement grew, so did Black self-liberation groups.

There was a real pressure sweeping across the trade union movement during the 1980s and 90s for Black workers to make a clean break with the existing trade union movement and to create Black trade unions.

It was a genuine debate put forward primarily by Black nationalists who never really wanted to work within the institutions of the labour movement anyway.

They used the emerging Black union structures to push their nationalist beliefs off the back of a poor union record of tackling racism in the workplace.

The response of some TUC affiliates was to look at their own practices and procedures during the mid-1980s as more Black workers began to assert themselves for greater representation by and within their unions.

NALGO: The First "Official" Breakthrough

While most Black self-liberation structures within British unions, even up to today, are informal, and stronger for the level of independence it provides, the first "official," formal structures for Black union members were set up in local government union NALGO during the early 1980s.

It was in response to the failure of the union to deal with the issues facing Black workers in the workplace and in the union, particularly racial harassment and discrimination that Black workers began to informally organise together throughout the country.

The demand was for representation at all levels of the union to ensure that the organisation responded to the racism that was facing these Black workers.

The response from the NALGO leadership to the groundswell of dissatisfaction over representation and the racism being experienced by many of its Black members was to set up a Race Equality Working Party (REWP) in 1984.

Black workers in Nalgo disrupted the first meeting of the Working Party in central London when it became clear that there was to be no representation on the REWP for any of the informal groups that had already been established.

After the protest – and by securing the support of white anti-racists within the union – the Black activists secured agreement for the establishment of a form of black self-organisation or liberation within NALGO.

There are three critical points that need to be made.

Firstly, Black activists were always forced to struggle against the resistance of trade union leaderships to secure change.

The common experience was of initial resistance from union hierarchies to wider Black representation. It was not until much later (in the early 1990s) that unions started (albeit reluctantly) to more widely accept the need to provide formal structures for Black workers within their organisations.

Secondly, the structures that emerged were variations on the theme of self-liberation and were often some form of a hybrid between advisory to the ruling executive bodies and self-organised groupings.

Even while formal structures emerged Black workers continued to organise informally within the union.

Such organisations eventually spread across a large number of unions from the 1980s through to the 2000s in Britain across the public, private and voluntary sectors – often after initial hostility from white union leaderships.

But these communities of Black resistance to racism within trade unions did not rely on being formally recognised by the union hierarchy.

The overwhelming experience in Britain is of informal Black self-liberation structures emerging and flourishing within trade unions even where some form of structure and representation has been formally sanctioned by the union.

Thirdly, the winning of change by Black workers within unions also required the support of white anti-racists or sympathisers. This was, in fact, critical to change taking place.

The power bases within unions needed to be won to the principle of wider access and wider participation.

It was, after all, white workers that had control over the levers of power within unions. It was they that controlled the decision-making processes or could at least exert more influence over the political factions that controlled union hierarchies.

The relationships between Black and white union activists over issues of self-liberation or formal representation such as through reserved seats on union executive bodies or Black worker conferences was often uneasy and difficult even where those white activists were generally considered to be progressives.

The perceived location of the ruling group within the union as generally either being on the left politically or more right wing just seemed to mean that the tone and emphasis of the response to the demands by Black workers was different.

But the initial negative response for support, with few exceptions, was, however, somewhat the same.

Works on the location of power and, in particular union power are instructive here. Power structures within organisations, including unions, tend to try to replicate themselves to ensure their survival.

This being the case, unions with few if any Black workers in or near positions of power tended to continue to bring through white workers to replace outgoing leaders.

One of the many challenges facing Black trade union activists was how best to stem this tide and introduce a new direction and inject the Black radical tradition into the veins of a white-dominated movement.

The audacity of Black workers challenging the dominant structures within the trade union movement was not enough on its own to stir unions to respond. Indeed, these dominant structures were overwhelmingly conservative, guided by the traditionally dampening hand of the TUC.

This meant that the challenge by Black workers within some unions was sometimes labelled as being radical when, in reality, the only radical things being demanded were an end to discrimination by union officials, the same level of service for black workers as was received by whites (which wasn't always a great deal) and, perhaps most controversially, a seat at the union decision-making table through reserved seats.

The link to the Black radical tradition is far more layered than these demands would suggest.

It was not until the critical mass of Black workers had reached a sufficient level within the movement and, especially, when the resistance to the existing order was organised in a way that reflected the tradition of Black radicalism, that progress began to be made in shifting the trade union movement.

Of course, this was not uniform across the trade union movement. Black workers made more ground in gaining employment in public services, such as local government and the health service, than anywhere else so, consequently, Black workers communities of resistance were most obviously stronger in those areas.

But regardless of where the organising was taking place against racism, Black workers drew on a radical tradition of resistance to help guide them through their battles.

The eventual responses from ruling union groupings

reflected the often uneasy relationship that existed between Black and white workers in attempting to forge a unified resistance to racism.

There were examples of Black and white workers coming together to resist racism in Britain.

For example the Co-ordinating Committee Against Racial Discrimination (CCARD).

CCARD was responsible for organising a march of Blacks and whites through the streets of Birmingham in September 1961 in a demonstration against the Immigration Bill of that time.

But, there was little evidence of this cooperation between collective Black voices and trade unions.

Only the IWA, even with its Communist links, really commanded the respect of the white leaders of the trade union movement.

This could perhaps be because the IWA had a proven track record of delivering members for the trade union movement – an understandable (to some extent) preoccupation that seemed to outweigh any other considerations with most trade unions well into the 1990s.

The organisation of formal Black workers structures in other unions, besides Nalgo, was somewhat eclectic.

Very few of the formal structures that developed during the 1980s could remotely be described as self-organised or having very much to do with liberation.

At least there was a mixed record of success in delivering any significant change on the ground to deal with the racism still being experienced by Black workers.

They were a mix of advisory-type committees to the national structures of unions and hybrids of limited self-organisation and advisory. The structures that emerged depended to a large extent on what Black activists were able to negotiate with union hierarchies and, arguably more importantly, controlling factions.

Ultimately the question was how far controlling elements within unions were willing to provide routes to power for Black activists. The answer was, as it always is, about political power.

If Black workers were prepared to deliver votes to ensure controlling factions within unions maintained their power they were far more likely to be fed a few more crumbs from the table.

It was also more likely that any Black person able to deliver these goods would be allowed to join the top table of union executives or granted a place on delegations to bodies such as the Congress of the TUC or Labour Party.

Labour Party Black Sections

During the 1970s, a time of Black industrial struggle and transition from a Keynesian, pluralistic society to the Friedmanite unitarist philosophy that eschewed any ideas of social partnership or collectivism, the Black community began to feel more under siege.

This siege mentality also fostered a belief that there were few options for the Black community towards which they could turn for support. The feeling of being under siege was also fed by the continuous harassment experienced by the Black community at the hands of the State through such policies as Stop and Search (SUS).

The only practical option for the Black community was to look to each other for support.

Activists that had been involved, in one way or another in some of the disputes of the 1970s or who had brought their own experiences of resistance to colonial rule began to organise.

This experience alongside the new energy provided by British-born Black activists, the predominantly second-generation descendants of the post-war immigrants to Britain, was a volatile cocktail.

It was a link between the older more established ways of organising derived from resisting the Empire and the specific African and Asian British experience.

As well as independent Black political organising, which was well established through organisations such as the Race Today Collective and the New Beacon Circle, there was a push to ensure that those mainstream organisations that had received overwhelming support from the Black community, namely the Labour Party and the trade union movement, now reciprocated.

During the early 1980s the trade union movement held a greater say over Labour Party policy and organisation than they do today. At that time, before the introduction of one member-one vote under John Smith leadership, the trade union block vote was still the dominant decision-making mechanism within the Labour Party.

To make progress within the Labour Party it was therefore vital to shift trade union attitudes.

The Labour Party Black Sections (LPBS) held its founding conference in London in 1983.

Linda Bellos, the former Black Sections activist and, later, leader of the London Borough of Lambeth Council, said: "When we started the black section of the Labour Party in 1983, we saw it as a struggle for representation for African, Caribbean and Asian voters and members of the Labour Party."[29]

As became more common in later years, the question of who could take part in the "unofficial" Black Sections was a point of debate.

Black, for the LPBS, was taken in an extremely broad context. While remaining, essentially, a self-definition, women and men of African, Caribbean and Asian descent came together with people of Palestinian and even Greek and Turkish Cypriot backgrounds to argue for greater representation within the Labour Party.

Labour Party Black Sections (LPBS)

29. L. Bellos, *Catalyst*, 25 May 2006.

The rules of the national LPBS were silent on who qualified for membership.

The objects of the LPBS said the main aim of the organisation was:

> "To fight to eliminate racism in the Labour Party and Labour movement, both institutional and personal, and to support black workers in their struggle against racism both in Britain and abroad".

So as well as being concerned with the national political scene the LPBS were committed, in the Black radical tradition, to a transnational approach to resisting racism.

LPBS always identified with African liberation struggles (particularly in South Africa), Palestine and the Aborigine cause in Australia.

The LPBS also, controversially, and much to the annoyance of the Labour Party leadership, organised a delegation to West Belfast to meet with Gerry Adams and other Sinn Fein officials.

The LPBS national rules were also written in such a way as to anticipate recognition by the Labour Party. For example, rule 2.b lists a broad object to "advise the National Executive Committee of the Labour Party". While rule 2.b (v) broadens the mandate to cover "any matters upon the request of the Labour Party National Executive Committee."

Despite its criticisms of the Labour Party the LPBS were Party loyalists – even though it was clear that many activists showed a far greater allegiance to organisations such as the Communist Party.

Rule 2.c underlined this commitment by saying that the LPBS existed to "secure the support of

Black people for the principles and policies of the
Labour Party".

From the beginning the purpose of the Black
Sections was not, as it is sometimes portrayed,
just about placing middle-class Black members of
the Labour Party into more influential positions
in the movement.

The LPBS was centrally concerned with policy
and even published a "Black Agenda" for the
Labour Party.

Having relied on the electoral support of the Black
community for many years Black section activists
believed that the Labour Party had failed to put in
place policies, locally or nationally, that did anything
to address the racism being suffered.

Winning more representation would mean that the
Black agenda for change would have more of an
opportunity to be implemented.

The Black Sections slammed the Labour Party
for failing to represent the interests of the Black
community. It was a view they shared with other
Black activists outside the Party.

There was a difference of opinion over whether the
Labour Party was ever going to treat the fight against
racism in more than just a superficial manner.

The view from outside the Labour Party was that
this was something that only independent Black
political organising could achieve.

This difference of opinion and approach was to
continually dog the relationship between Black
activists within and outside the Labour Party.

It would also be a mistake to believe that everyone within the LPBS shared the same political philosophy.

This was far from the case. The politics of those within the LPBS ranged across the spectrum from Marxist to Nationalists to Social Democrats to those fiercely loyal to the Labour Party to some who would never have joined with a gun at their head.

It was, in fact, a perfect example of the principles of a Black community of resistance to racism.

The point of unity for these activists was a common understanding that "Black", in this context, was (and is) a political movement and not a literal description.

There were sharp political debates within LPBS but no argument that the Labour Party was the main recipient of Black support in Britain – this was self-evident – and that it had consistently failed to deliver.

The only way to change this was to have more Black people involved as representatives, in the decision-making processes and, most of all, in the delivery of a Black agenda for radical change to tackle racism.

Its biggest success was the 1987 election of four of its members to Parliament.

Diane Abbott became the first elected Black woman MP when she was elected to Hackney North and Stoke Newington, Paul Boateng won in Brent South, Bernie Grant in Tottenham, and Keith Vaz in Leicester East.

Bernie Grant

Paul Boateng

Keith Vaz

Diane Abbott

Even with these successes the official recognition of Black Sections by the Labour Party remained elusive.

The strategy to change the Labour Party required changing the trade unions. Only a small number of unions affiliated to the party had consistently supported the LPBS cause.

The small Association of Cinematograph, Television and Allied Technicians (ACTT), now part of the Broadcasting, Entertainment, Cinematograph and Theatre Union (BECTU) - now a section of Prospect – was one of the first affiliated unions to give support to the movement for Black Sections.

However, there were few other unions that gave initial support to the Black Sections campaign.

The unions that did support Black Sections included NUPE and the National Union of Mineworkers.

Even though the movement for Black Sections within the Labour Party had significant support from the constituency parties this was going to be nowhere near enough to change the mind or position of the leadership of the Labour Party.

Decision-making in these pre-Blair days was conducted on an electoral college basis that was split evenly three ways between unions, constituencies and Members of Parliament.

Clearly, more unions needed to be persuaded to give support.

The usual lobbying of the leadership and their key officials by Black Sections activists had failed to make concrete inroads, other than expressions of sympathy on the left of the party, and (sometimes) friendly expressions of regret on the right, another tactic was required.

The author, as the LPBS trade union officer, was charged by the executive committee in 1988 with developing a new strategy for moving the position of trade unions.

The strategy was to maximise the efforts to develop Black self-organised formations within trade unions – particularly in those affiliated to the Labour Party.

The Black Trade Unionist Forum was launched at a conference in Wood Green, North London, on Saturday 10 February 1990 – the day before Nelson Mandela was released from his Cape Town prison in South Africa.

The conference was attended by around 100 Black trade unionists from 14 different unions. Most unions represented were from the public sector – which was a reflection of the strength of Black public sector employment and trade unionism.

The main purpose of the forum was "to support and facilitate the development of Black self-organised groups within trade unions". (Black Sections internal paper February 1990) The further aims of the forum were:

■ To liaise and communicate with Black self-organised groups within trade unions which operate at local, regional or a national level.

■ To provide a forum and/or opportunities for Black trade unionists to discuss self-organisation and associated issues of common concern.

■ To facilitate and encourage the involvement of Black trade unionists from a broad geographical spectrum.

■ To promote and ensure the implementation of an anti-racist and equal opportunities approach to the structure, operation and activities undertaken by the organisation.

■ To liaise with relevant bodies and individuals in order to promote Black self-organisation within trade unions.

■ To act as an information resource.

The BTUF founding conference, rather than discussing motions, used the day to hear from the experiences of a range of Black activists within their unions trying to either build self-organised groups or, at least, attempting to raise issues of anti-racism within their unions.

Primarily the messages were the same. Black workers were at the bottom of the pile, facing discrimination at work and indifference from their unions. It was an indifference to the plight of Black workers in the workplace as well as to their call for increased representation within their unions.

There was a clear understanding by those present that the time for change was not only at hand but that the architects of that change would be Black workers themselves.

It was agreed that the change required needed to be codified and so the conference attendees agreed to work towards the following 9 point plan (a Black Sections initiative even though many at the conference would never have dreamt of joining the Labour Party):

I   Rule changes to recognise the establishment of Black members groups where Black members want them.

II   Rule changes to facilitate an annual national meeting/conference of Black members.

III   Rule changes to provide reserved seats for Black members at all decision-making levels of union structures.

IV   The reserved seats for Black members to be elected by Black members only.

V   Reserved seats on any delegation from the union, including all levels of both the Labour Party and the TUC.

VI   Delegations to both the TUC and Labour Party Conferences to be determined on the basis of at least one Black delegate per 10 delegation seats (or part thereof) available.

VII The Black delegates to be elected by Black members only.

VIII Trade unions to appoint a Black members officer to head a Race Equality Department that has a national remit and provides additional support for Black members groups.

IX TUC to form a Race Equality Department separate completely from dealing with other issues of equality.[30]

One item that was added to the list during the conference was the need to have a meaningful TUC Black Workers Conference.

Up to that time the TUC conference had been little more than a seminar with a string of notable speakers gracing the platform and delegates being split into groups for discussions around a range of employment-related issues.

The demand came for a Black workers conference organised by the TUC that enabled some democratic input into union affairs. The call was for a motion-based conference of Black workers.

A small group of BTUF activists from NALGO, the National Union of Journalists (NUJ), the National Union of Civil and Public Servants (NUCPS) and the National Association of Teachers in Further and Higher Education (NATFHE – now part of the University and College Lecturers Union), met in 1991 to discuss democratising the TUC Black Workers Conference.

---

30. Internal Black Sections document, 1989.

This was a group of Black – in this case African – activists who were involved in setting up and developing Black self-liberation groups within their own unions coming together in the understanding that it was not possible to make progress in their separate organisations alone.

There needed to be a groundswell of pressure applied across the trade union movement as a whole and this meant using the existing set piece annual TUC conference for Black workers – really a seminar where the great and the good were given the opportunity to say how bad racism was – in a way that actually empowered Black workers.

The 1992 Congress agreed to a motion-based Black workers conference. This at least gave delegates an opportunity to share the examples of the racism that was being experienced across a range of sectors but, most importantly, setting unions the task of coming up with strategies for challenging racism and being held accountable for it by Black workers.

BTUF was, to put it mildly, a very ambitious project, but, as with many Black political self-organised groupings, it was a very short-lived. However, the forum served an important purpose in helping to identify a Black agenda for activists within trade unions and provided an important stimulus for the Black worker trade union organisations that were to emerge over the next decade.

The LPBS itself was instrumental to the establishment of the Labour Party Black Socialist Society (BSS) in 1993.

The BSS has representation on the National Executive Committee of the Labour Party (one of the key demands of LPBS) and an annual conference where policy can be debated and officers elected.

The work in the trade unions while critical in bringing about the votes necessary to achieve Black representation in the Labour Party the agitation of activists within LPBS was the most central.

The Importance of African Self-Liberation Strategies

This chapter illustrates how racism must be understood as an instrument of exploitation in the workplace and beyond.

Far from being an abstract phenomenon of ideas and influences, racism is a dynamic which is deeply rooted in the structures of exploitation, power and privilege.

Consequently the radical tradition of resistance to racism by African and Asian workers through the creation of communities of resistance is also far from being random or accidental. It is often literally a matter of life and death.

At the root of this resistance is the link between race and class. To treat them as completely irrelevant to each other, as I have suggested elsewhere in this book, is to weaken the struggle against both class and racial inequality as well as the fight for socialism.

Racism is determined by the ruling class in order to protect its own interests and race discrimination, direct or indirect, has always been closely tied to both employment and political considerations.

That is why we must always maintain a clear focus on the role of racism in the sharpest arena in the conflict that exists between capital and labour – that of the workplace.

If we accept the central role of racism in the fight between capital and labour then, for me, it follows that socialists must treat seriously the need for anti-racist action to be central to our work.

This does not mean just reiterating how long you have been an anti-racist without any demonstrable evidence to prove it.

The fact that an activist might have once read something by Angela Davis or Claudia Jones or that you or your parents might have a love for the music and activity of Paul Robeson simply will not cut it for Black workers.

Neither does it mean ignoring the central role that Black workers must play in deciding how best to go about winning our own liberation.

We are under racist attack and have been for the entirety of my lifetime and for many generations before my parents were even born.

Black people want collaborators in the fight against racism rather than just warm words of commitment that we are supposed to just accept on trust.

Black and white workers predominantly occupy the same place in society – a society dominated by capital.

Whilst we share the same working-class interests we are forced by the monopolist minority to compete with each other for limited resources – which leads to racism.

It also leads to the need to find ways of resisting racism through such strategies as Black self-organisation as well as in united Black and white anti-racist organisations.

I do not believe that Black self-liberation divides the

working class as a number of white comrades have attempted to convince me.

I take the view that it is a platform from which we can build class consciousness which, in turn, can strengthen the working class – from which we are often excluded as being a core component.

I believe that it is a fundamental mistake to reduce race to class but also an error of the highest proportions to try to understand class without race.

I do not suggest for a moment that everyone involved in Black self-liberation formations is knowingly or even willingly taking part in class struggle.

You don't have to believe that you are engaging in the class struggle to take part – no more than it is necessary to believe in the theory of relativity to fall from an aeroplane.

Black workers, like other workers, are forced to struggle against the excesses of capital from necessity.

For Black workers the added immediate ingredient to be resisted is racism. To not resist racism or class exploitation would be, in my opinion, to acquiesce to it.

The act of resistance to racism takes on the form of a wider resistance to class oppression.

This is why white resistance to racism becomes a necessity.

Without white workers resisting racism the working class remains divided and in a therefore weaker position in the conflict with capital.

We should resist, as the legendary African American communist Henry Winston once said, a "skin strategy" for resisting racism. I take this to mean that it is not only Black workers who must resist racism.

To reduce African self-liberation to this level is deeply insulting. Unfortunately it is the hallmark of many who describe themselves as anti-racist but who do little to prove it beyond giving fine speeches in a room full of self-congratulatory people.

While I believe that it is in the vital interests of the working class to unite against racism, African self-liberation has played a central role in cultivating the ground for the growth of the necessary unity.

Without African self-liberation through communities of resistance, I am doubtful that anti-racism would have been high enough up the agenda – even in many parts of the left – for anything meaningful to happen.

Black self-liberation within trade unions in Britain provides a distinct dynamic that contributes to the development of class unity to resist both racism and class exploitation.

This is not to minimise the worth of other forms of self-liberation outside of trade unions. But unions play a particular and vital role in building working class resistance.

Workplace resistance to racism by Black workers cannot be divorced from the activities that were (and are) taking place elsewhere such as in political parties, international solidarity, community campaigns, access to public services such as education and housing as well as in campaigns against the various resurgences of the far right.

There is an organic link between these areas of activity, with many of the same people involved in Black self-organisation within trade unions taking an active role in these other campaigns.

The important role of the Black sections movement in the Labour Party to the creation and development of Black communities of resistance in trade unions is far too often underplayed, as is the unique contribution made by the Indian Workers Association.

The fight against racism was and is being waged in a multi-layered way and all fronts by Black workers.

Not least of which is the internationalist dimension to the struggle against racism – indivisible, in many ways, from the struggle taking place in the belly of the beast itself.

Whether through education, housing or by seeking access to goods and services such as mortgages, racism was and is being resisted by Black workers, usually by self-organised means.

The left should be celebrating Black self-organisation, not criticising these vital communities of resistance against racism.

The task is to find ways of making sure that socialist theory is deeply embedded in a way that will ensure it leads to revolutionary practice.

Foreign Ministry of the Republic of Indonesia, *Conference poster of the Bandung Conference*, 1955

CHAPTER THREE
The transnational fight for African Freedom

Introduction

Building communities of resistance for Africans has always been an international endeavour – almost by definition.

The links to the Mother Continent have always remained strong after enslavement and colonialism.

Wherever Africans have found themselves across the diaspora – whether by choice or by force – we have defined ourselves in relation to Africa.

Africans across the diaspora have internationalism as a default position. This is not just in relation to the African continent.

It helps to explain why Africans have little difficulty in offering solidarity to other oppressed peoples of the world, such as the Palestinians – because we too have been displaced and exploited.

A number of global bodies have played key roles in helping Africans across the diaspora to build communities of resistance towards African liberation.

This chapter looks at a few of these. Whilst not exhaustive these are some of the bodies that I believe have understood African agency in our own liberation.

Given the legacy of militant labour unrest in the run-up to the war there must have been considerable concern by the British about the reaction of the colonised population should hostilities break out after the so-called "phoney war".

Gerald Horne goes so far as to suggest that "London

– and its erstwhile ally, Washington – had a security problem in the Caribbean."[31]

Nowhere was this more the case than in Jamaica and Trinidad and Tobago, in the Caribbean.

The islands of the Caribbean were a particularly important consideration during World War II.

The cheap labour available in the region was going to be important in supporting the war effort of the US and, therefore, the rest of the Allies.

Indeed, the increased connection of the Caribbean with the US before and during the war was to have a profound effect on the shape of future international relations.

The British were to find it increasingly difficult to hang on to these spoils of Empire as the US began to increase their sphere of influence to include the British "possessions" as part of what began to become known as "their backyard".

The mere fact of the existence of cheap labour for the war effort and the possible future exploitation of some of the natural resources of the region could not mask the difficulties that existed in both the US and the ruling British maintaining control.

Jamaica, in particular, was seen as a security problem because of its history of labour unrest – particularly after the major labour rebellion of 1938.

Trinidad and Tobago was a problem for similar reasons to Jamaica but also because of its important oil fields – vital for the war effort.

---

31. G. Horne, *Cold War in a Hot Zone: The United States Confronts Labour and Independence Struggles in the British West Indies*, Temple University Press, Philadelphia, 2007, p.41.

India, because of the activities and successes of the liberation movement, under the inspirational leadership of Gandhi, had been a problem for the British Empire for some considerable time.

India, in particular, was a key barometer for how the rest of the colonies were to be treated during the war. Indeed, as Nigel Bolland points out: "What was happening in the bigger colonies, such as India, Ceylon, Kenya and Nigeria, had more impact on the imperial system, and hence on the smaller colonies such as those in the Caribbean, than vice versa."[32]

Typically, the British were to respond to the perceived security threat in the only way that they knew, which was to intern the leaders of resistance in the hope that this would stem the resistance.

However, the wartime internment of the leaders of Black resistance to Empire predictably failed, as it always had done, to quell the tide of Black workers demanding their rights to equality and justice. The colonial rulers had not addressed the causes of the labour rebellions of 1938, particularly those that occurred in Jamaica.

Between 1934 and 1939 a series of labour rebellions swept across the region. The Great Depression of the 1930s, which had had such a devastating effect on the World economy, was a catastrophe for the monocrop economies of the Caribbean.

This presented more fertile ground for the spreading of influences such as Garveyism and Marxism across the region. If the rulers of the Empire did not appear to care about the fate of the people of the region – who

---

32. O. Nigel Bolland, *The Politics of Labour in the British Caribbean*, James Currey, Oxford, 2001.

saw their already meagre, predominantly agricultural, living disappear and the daily grind of existing poverty deepening and becoming yet more widespread – then, something else was needed.

That something else, it seemed to many people, was to follow Garveyism or Marxism and certainly to rebel against what was already on offer – grinding poverty.

The backbone of support for Garveyism during this period was, at least initially, amongst migrant workers returning home from working away during the more prosperous 1920s.

On being forced to return home, once work opportunities were closed in places such as the US and Cuba, many of these migrant workers, while swelling the already large ranks of the unemployed, had gained some experience of trade unionism.

Many had certainly come into contact with or been influenced by the Garvey movement.

The depth of the feeling against the British rulers was profound.

One can judge the depth of feeling from the testimony of Albert Gomes, the Trinidadian leader. Gomes reported that he witnessed Black cinema audiences generously cheering newsreel appearances, at various times, of Hitler, Mussolini and Stalin.

While there is little evidence to corroborate the testimony of Gomes it does seem hard to believe that there would not have been some local reaction by locals to the treatment they received from the colonial rulers and the extremely harsh economic circumstances that prevailed at the time.

If Gomes is correct it also seems to be an extreme record of what has become known as the "anyone but England" concept.

Whatever Gomes heard from cinema audiences, the feelings certainly ran deeper than hostility towards the British alone. There was also a deal of anti-Americanism.

This had been born from a direct experience, by Blacks in the British Caribbean, of Jim Crow white supremacy in two ways.

Firstly, there was the treatment that migrant workers had endured during their stay in the US and, secondly, the attitudes and behaviour of some Americans towards the local population when US bases were being built in the Caribbean.

Not surprisingly the anti-Americanism and the growing anti-colonial feeling led to outward expressions of frustration and rebellion in the Caribbean islands during the war years.

This frustration was fed by the knowledge that while some men from the Caribbean went off to fight with distinction in the war the lot of many more was to provide the cheap and moveable labour necessary to maintain the war effort.

Black workers were moved around the Caribbean to work on the mushrooming US bases and into mainland USA itself. The only obstacle to the movement of labour was the heightened German U-Boat campaign in the region.

In fact by the end of the war the actions of the U-Boats had crippled the Caribbean economy and created virtual starvation conditions on the islands.

The movement of these Black workers across the region and, indeed, the experience of the Black servicemen, had a profound influence. As Horne (2007) describes the experience:

".... exposed them to stimulating experiences as it enhanced their internationalism and reduced their provincialism, making them more susceptible to regional forms of organisation."[33]

It was certainly not beyond the wit of Black workers to understand that the freedom they were being enjoined to fight for, either as service personnel or as labourers for the cause, was not something they currently experienced or one that, unless things changed, they were destined to experience.

If freedom was on offer then Black workers, from all parts of the Empire, who heard the same Churchillian rhetoric as everyone else, wanted a piece of the action.

The only question facing Black workers across the Empire was how to improve their lot. After all, the 1930s depression had already taken a significant toll on the economy of the region, as it had everywhere else, and the effective blockading of the islands by German U-Boats during the war had only made things worse. Unemployment was high and food was scarce. Times were extremely hard.

Eric Williams, in his classic work on the history of the Caribbean (1970), documents the detrimental effects of insufficient and deficient food in the period leading up to the war.

---

33. Horne, *Cold War in a Hot Zone*, p.56.

Williams for example quotes a report from a committee on nutrition in Barbados during 1936 as saying: "The diet of the average worker can be classed at best only as a maintenance diet, and…there is no reason to doubt that many households live on the borderland of extreme poverty."[34]

Looking beyond the immediate necessity to survive was a difficult prospect but, as always, desperate times call for desperate measures. The desperate measures called for were the collective forms of resistance that had always been called on by Black workers. Although largely written out of history, the 1930s were times of major industrial unrest in the Caribbean Islands.

The situation was so appalling during the early 1930s for Black workers that, for example, in Port of Spain, the capital of Trinidad, a hunger march was organised by a group called the National Unemployed Movement.

Trinidad 1930s

34. E. Williams, *From Columbus to Castro: The History of the Caribbean. 1492-1969*, Andre Deutsch Ltd., London, 1970.

This was the first of a wave of demonstrations – a number of others taking place on sugar estates across the island.

Workers loading bananas at Oracabessa in St. Mary, Jamaica on 13 May 1935 went on strike and blocked access roads to stop strikebreakers from being brought in.

Eight days later there was a strike of dockworkers at Falmouth in Trelawny. Workers rose up when the owners sought to bring in strikebreakers and when a striker was shot dead by the police.

There were further strikes in the capital Kingston during 1935. One was a strike of banana loaders. Once again the police opened fire on the strikers.

In June 1935 the Jamaica Permanent Development Convention, a Garveyist organisation, held a public meeting at which it announced plans for the formation of a trade union.

Nothing came of this proposal but, in May 1936, the Jamaica Workers and Tradesmen's Union was launched with A G S Coombs as President and Hugh Clifford Buchanan as Secretary. Buchanan was, according to Hart, Jamaica's first active Marxist.

On July 28, in Barbados, the lightermen went on strike. They only returned to work on August 4, when their demands were met, but there were still sporadic strikes and threats of strikes in several other workplaces.

In reflex mode, the Government acted ruthlessly in suppressing the accompanying disorder – ordering the armed police into crowds.

These were examples of the ferment that was sweeping across the Caribbean during this period. It meant two things for our purposes.

Firstly, when the call came from Britain to defend "freedom" against the Nazis the response was, at best, a questioning one and, at worst, a hostility.

Blacks in the Caribbean were, in effect, being asked to defend more of the same sort of treatment that they had endured for generations.

Secondly, the wave of rebellion across the Caribbean and, importantly, how to organise, was an experience that was not forgotten when Black workers migrated to the UK in the post-war years.

Rather than arriving in Britain as a blank sheet of paper, Black workers actually brought a wealth of organising experience and a clear understanding of what decent treatment at work and beyond actually meant.

African Resistance across the Empire

There is a penetrating silence that greets talk of the existence of any African resistance to colonial rule.

Little attention has been paid to the resistance that was rife across the West Indies and in parts of Africa.

Without the immense efforts of writers such as Hart (1988, 1989, 1997, 1998), and Nigel Bolland (1995, 2001), this important legacy of resistance would have been easily lost.

The resistance to the British Empire at home was mirrored by what was taking place overseas. These two sides of the resistance were characterised by activists who straddled both arenas.

This was to become a recurring theme in later years when the boundaries between the resistances against racism at home and abroad were to become increasingly blurred.

At this time of great international upheaval and world revolution (Russia in 1917) these activists found their own way to resist colonialism and racism and paved the way for others in the Black diaspora.

The exploitation of the local population by the agents of British imperialism and their use of repressive force led to violent resistance from the colonial working class across the colonies.

Trinidad, for example, was the scene of violent resistance to colonial repression during 1919. The roots of these troubles began in 1917 with the abolition of the indentured labour system for East Indians.

This then produced a shortage of labour. The unemployed were permitted by the rather notorious Habitual Idlers Ordinance to be used as chattel.

Buhle (1988) tells of how "Longshoreman struck warehouses in mid-December 1918, driving scabs from the premises.

"Their march through Port of Spain shut down the city in December 1919 and offered an object lesson in what a later generation would call Black Power."[35]

These events were a precursor to a later series of strikes, uprisings and labour disturbances that swept through the English-speaking Caribbean in the 1930s, beginning in Belize (British Honduras), Trinidad, and Guyana in 1934, and culminating in Jamaica in 1938, and Antigua and Guyana in 1939.

35. P. Buhle, *CLR James: Artist as Revolutionary*, Verso, London, 1988, p.24.

There were also labour uprisings in St Kitts, St Vincent, St Lucia, Barbados, and the Bahamas during this period.

These acts of rebellion against British imperialism were products of a constant and more low-level resistance to racism played out on a daily basis as a result of the systematic economic exploitation experienced by those living under colonial rule.

The rise in militancy by African workers in the British Caribbean was not in isolation from events taking place worldwide during the early part of the twentieth century but it was still only in Russia that workers had managed to seize power from the ruling imperial class and maintain it.

St Kitts 1930s

Guyana 1930s

The Communist International

Revolution or, at the very least, a desire for change from the old pre- Great War order was in the air. It was also at the very epicentre of what Davis, when referring to the period between 1910 and 1926, called "the most revolutionary phase of the history of the British labour movement".[36]

The uprisings and disturbances, both in Britain and abroad, should not be seen in solely simplistic racial terms. While racism was clearly an important factor it was not the only one.

These events must be analysed on a number of different levels. After all, it was only two years earlier in 1917 that the earthquake of the Russian revolution took place.

The Russian revolution was clearly not an issue of race but it was certainly heavily influenced by anti-imperialism.

The revolution in Russia took place at a time when the desire for radical change was taking hold across the world – not least in the colonies of the British Empire.

This decisive blow against the seemingly impregnable imperial powers gave hope to countless onlookers who, perhaps for the first time, were able to see that change was indeed possible.

1919, almost as if to reinforce the year as a beacon in the pantheon of revolutionary struggle, also saw the founding of the Communist International Comintern in Moscow.

---

36. M. Davis, *Sylvia Pankhurst, A Life in Radical Politics*, Pluto Press, London, 1999, p.102.

The first Congress of the Comintern, held between March 2 and 6, was a predominantly white European affair although there were some representatives from China and Korea.

Although there were no representatives at the first Congress from either Africa, India or the Caribbean, the Comintern went on, in later years, to develop a clear anti-imperialist project.

Indeed Lenin, the chief architect of both the revolution and the Comintern had completed one of his major works, *Imperialism, The Highest Stage of Capitalism*, some three years earlier in 1916.

In this work, Lenin went beyond the traditional notions of imperialism as exploitation of colonies to exploit raw materials.

He saw imperialism as a transitional stage towards a new "parasitic" stage of capitalism in which "advanced, wealthy nations would dominate underdeveloped, poor nations by the simple device of exporting capital."[37]

---

37. V. Lenin, 'Imperialism, the Highest Stage of Capitalism', 1916 in H. M. Christman, *Essential Works of Lenin: What is to be done? and other writings*, Dover publications, New York, 1966.

Lenin's view of the nature of imperialism is important for our understanding of the development and operation of colonialism as well as how the resistance to its foundational racism grew into modes of Black self-liberation.

It has also proven to be entirely correct in the way that the former colonial powers continue to pillage natural resources such as cobalt and uranium from the Global South to keep the rich nations in the manner to which they have become accustomed.

The politics of imperial Britain was decisive in shaping events at both home and abroad, which, in turn, shaped the nature of the resistance to both the Empire and the daily experience of racism.

This should not be taken to signify that resisting racism was at the forefront of the concerns of the left during this period. Internationally, it took the Comintern until 1922 to adopt its *Theses on the Negro Question*, while in Britain, as Davis points out, "very few debates in the left press on the issue of racism" took place during this period.[38]

The first Congress of the Communist International Comintern

---

38. Davis, *Sylvia Pankhurst*, p.102.

The link between the heady debates around imperialism and the day-to-day reality of racism at home and abroad clearly had not reached the consciousness of left circles in Britain.

China at its world congresses in the early 1920s, the Atlantic world and especially sub-Saharan Africa remained a blank spot on the world-map of the forthcoming World Revolution.

Although John Reed vehemently called upon the comrades to focus on the downtrodden Black population in the US in a famous speech at the Second World Congress in Moscow in 1920, the Comintern was slow to develop a distinctive strategy for agitation and propaganda among the Black working class in the Atlantic world.

At first, the Comintern addressed only the conditions of the Black working class in the US and in South Africa in the so-called 'Negro Theses' of 1922 and 1924; the situation in the African colonies, in the Caribbean or in Latin America (especially Brazil) remained marginal if recognised at all.

A similar case was the 1920 *Theses on the National and Colonial Question* that heavily criticised British and French imperialism in sub-Saharan Africa and the Caribbean, and had placed the metropolitan parties in the West in the forefront for orchestrating anti-colonial and anti-imperial agitation and propaganda.

However, one of the biggest dilemmas for the architects of the Communist anti-colonial doctrine was an apparent lack of left-wing militant agents for leading the anti-colonial struggle in the African and Caribbean colonies.

Those who were around tended to be Black intellectuals

and "petty-bourgeois anti-colonial nationalists" who tended towards a radical Pan-Africanism as their ideology rather than communism.

Initially, Moscow's tactical considerations included a temporary alliance between the communists and the anti-colonial nationalists in colonial and 'semi-colonial' countries as set out by Lenin's thesis on the National and Colonial Question.

In contrast to the social democrats and the Labour and Socialist International, the rhetoric of the Comintern and the communists was in its essence anti-imperial and anti-colonial, calling for the national independence of the colonies and fully backing the struggle against capitalist and colonial exploitation.

The rationale of communist doctrines positioned US African radicals-cum-communists in the vanguard of anti-colonial and anti-imperial agitation and propaganda in the Black Atlantic.

Africans from the Caribbean and Africa were largely marginal to the debate.

However, the ultra-left turn and the introduction of the "Class-Against-Class" doctrine of the Comintern and the Red International of Labour Unions (RILU) in 1928 terminated any existing cooperation with African radical nationalists.

Instead, radical international proletarian solidarity demanded cooperation between the Black and white working class and the new doctrine called for a new approach for the radicalisation of workers throughout the Black Atlantic.

This was materialised in the establishment of the International Trade Union Committee of Negro

Workers in July 1928; its key initial organiser being the African American communist trade union organiser James W. Ford.

Ford was key in reframing the work of the ITUCNW among colonial seamen and putting their concerns on the agenda of the international left movement.

But one person, George Padmore, did as much as any, if not more, to build the African international resistance to racism.

George Padmore

George Padmore played a central role in developing and building transnational African liberation communities of resistance.

Born Malcolm Nurse in Trinidad during June of 1903, he changed his name, as did many (particularly communist) activists of the time, as cover from identification while involved in clandestine activities.

As a university activist student in the United States in the 1920s, Padmore joined the Communist Party and quickly rose in its ranks.

Padmore became one of the leading African activists within the Communist International - known as the Comintern.

He became chair of the RILU and the executive secretary of the International Trade Union Committee of Negro Workers (ITUCNW).

Padmore was responsible for organising an elaborate

network of thousands of anti-colonial militants throughout the Caribbean and Africa during the Great Depression.

George Padmore

There were five objectives of the ITUCNW set out at a conference held in Hamburg in July 1930:

I To carry on propaganda and agitation, calling upon the negro workers to organise themselves into revolutionary trade unions in order to fight for higher wages, shorter hours and better conditions.

II To help the millions of negro workers who are now unemployed organise councils in order to demand relief from their government, free rent and non-payment of taxes.

III To agitate and organise the negro workers against the approaching imperialist war and the intervention in Soviet Russia, in which the white capitalist exploiters intend to use Black workers as cannon fodder as they did in the last war.

IV To promote and develop the spirit of international solidarity between workers of all colours and nationalities, calling upon them to support the Soviet Union which fights for the freedom of the working class and all oppressed peoples, as well as the Chinese, Indian, South African and all other revolutionary movements of the colonial toilers.

V The Committee also fights against white chauvinism, social reformism and the reformist programmes of the negro capitalist misleaders, like Marcus Garvey, Du Bois, Pickens and Walter White of the National Association of Coloured People in America; Kadalie and Champion in South Africa, the white trade union faker, Captain Cipriani, in the West Indies; and the missionaries, preachers and other agents of imperialism.

The Hamburg conference was originally due to be held in London but once they got wind of the event the Labour government of Ramsey MacDonald refused to allow it to take place in Britain.

But there was another problem. There appears to have been little help from the Communist Party of Britain in organising the conference.

Authorities across Europe and South Africa created roadblocks to the participation of the conference delegates by denying passports and visas as well as threatening to arrest anyone attending the conference.

Some 17 delegates from the African continent, the West Indies, the US and Latin America attended the conference. There is no record of anyone from Britain having attended.

One can only speculate over whether holding the conference in London, notwithstanding the obstacles mentioned above, might have given a spur to more African involvement in the communist movement in Britain.

On one level this was, after all, an African self-liberation project and so needed to be led by Africans. But on another, assistance with local logistics would have been more than helpful.

The organising committee of the Hamburg conference was M. Ali, William Burroughs, M.E Burns, James Ford, Otto Hall, Johnstone (Jomo) Kenyatta, Isaac Munsey, Lucas Prentice, W Thibedi and Padmore. Ford was the chair of the committee.

In any case the delegates spoke about racism in the workplace, starvation wages, long hours and the terrible living conditions that most African workers were living in.

The conference formed a "permanent body," the Negro Workers Committee, so the delegates could maintain contact and coordinate future work. This is the committee referred to in point five of the aims of the ITUCNW.

Padmore was clear that the committee, despite its name, was "not a race, but a class organisation, organising and leading the fight in the interests of negro workers in Africa, the West Indies and other colonies."

It was certainly a body rooted in class-based politics but it also reflected the understanding of the Comintern that there needed to be specific actions taken to resist the racism experienced by African workers.

Padmore was also the editor of the *Negro Worker* newspaper. This was one of the most important writing contributions that any African made for the Comintern.

The *Negro Worker* was the main organ used by the Comintern to win Africans to the revolutionary cause and also for African workers to use to build communities of resistance to racism on a local and transnational basis.

It must be said that this was not in addition to many other communist writings on racism for the duration of its existence between 1928 to 1937. There was actually precious little else.

Much of the writings on "race" across the international communist movement conflated fighting racism with anti-colonialism. Whilst being important relatives they are not the same thing.

I return to this issue in the final chapter because there is still an unfortunate and irritating tendency in the communist movement internationally to totally subsume the fight against racism as a fight against colonialism.

In *What is to Be Done?* Lenin said "a newspaper is not only a collective propagandist and a collective agitator, it is also a collective organiser."[39]

---

39. Lenin in H. M. Christman, *Essential Works of Lenin*, p.54.

It was therefore essential that any notion Padmore had of attempting to organise African workers on any level that he must write for a newspaper.

In his first editorial for the *Negro Worker* Padmore said his intention was for the paper to be a "theoretical journal." Understanding the need to reach as wide an African audience as he could Padmore, thankfully used it as much more of an organising tool.

After the first year of Padmore's editorship around 5000 copies were circulated in Africa – mainly South Africa – and across the West Indies despite attempts by the colonial powers to stop it.

The paper was essentially smuggled by a network of couriers to colonial ports.

But this did not prevent the paper from being banned in both Nigeria and Trinidad.

The paper was a vital source of information for African workers wherever they could get it.

Hearing about the struggles that others are experiencing is one of the cornerstones of the African self-liberation movement. One of the other cornerstones is the call to action.

The *Negro Worker* was a vital tool for both of these critical objectives during the nine-year life of the paper.

The nine-year existence of the paper should not be seen as a failure. Many political publications in these times of greater technological facility fail to last that long.

After breaking with Communism over their attitude to colonialism, Padmore returned to London with few resources. However, he managed to chart a course, which would deeply influence anti-colonialist movements in both Africa and the Caribbean.

Padmore established the International African Service Bureau, a network that coordinated voluminous correspondence between African and Caribbean nationalists, trade unionists, editors and intellectuals.

Padmore launched another publication, the *International African Opinion*, which emerged as an invaluable source of information and analysis for Black radicals.

Padmore was the mentor and influential theoretician to an entire generation of African leadership, including Jomo Kenyatta of Kenya and Kwame Nkrumah of Ghana.

It is difficult to over-emphasise Padmore's crucial ideological and political role in the emergence of political nationalism and movements of independence in English-speaking Africa.

Like Garvey, Padmore dreamt and worked for an independent Africa, united around the principles of mutual cooperation and Pan-Africanism.

However, his Pan-Africanist vision failed to fully recognise the power of British and French colonialists to co-opt independence movements, and to replace the white colonial elite with a new Black elite.

After Padmore left the Communist Party, he sadly became a bitter critic of Marxism. He argued in his 1955 book *Pan Africanism or Communism* that Black people must be "mentally free from the dictation of Europeans, regardless of their ideology."

Padmore's animus may have been somewhat based on his eventual acrimonious break from the Communist Party but underlying his argument above is the notion that Africans should not feel tied completely to Marxism and perhaps, in common with the Chinese today, should be free to pursue communism with "African characteristics."

Padmore committed his entire life to Black resistance to racism and Black liberation. After his death in September 1959, dozens of new independent states in the Caribbean and Africa would enter the world stage.

They owed their independence, in part, to the monumental contributions of Padmore through his relationship with both Nkrumah and Kenyatta.

In the UK the resistance to racism had its own history and its own dynamic. It was a resistance largely born from the experience of British colonial rule and, importantly, how to fight it.

As we see in later chapters African and other Black workers did not sit idly by and accept their lot under colonial rule. The resistance to colonial rule was fierce and was understood as and linked to the fight against racism. George Padmore played a critical role in helping to develop the transnational African radical tradition.

Marcus Garvey and the UNIA

Marcus Garvey was born in Jamaica on August 17 1887 and was best known for being the founder and leader of the Universal Negro Improvement Association and African Communities League (UNIA).

The UNIA was an international self-liberation organisation founded in Jamaica in 1914.

The UNIA saw extremely rapid growth. Garvey inaugurated the New York division of the UNIA in 1917 with 13 members. After only three months, the organisation's paying membership reached three thousand five hundred.

Garvey established the *Negro World* in January 1918, as a weekly newspaper to promote the ideas of the organisation.

Garvey's contribution to the newspaper was a front page editorial each week on a range of different issues of concern to him (and therefore to the UNIA).

Eventually claiming a circulation of five hundred thousand, it was printed in several languages, contained a page specifically for women, documented international events and was distributed throughout the African diaspora until it ceased publication in 1933.

In 1919 the UNIA purchased what would be the first of its numerous Liberty Halls. Located on 138th Street in New York City, the structure had a seating capacity of six thousand.

Later that year the UNIA organised the first of its two steamship companies and a separate business corporation. During the same year Garvey also founded the Black Star Line (BSL).

The proceeds from the highly successful stock sale of the company were used to buy three ships for its various commercial ventures.

The Negro Factories Corporation was also established in 1919.

The corporation generated income and provided jobs through its chain of grocery shops, restaurants, laundry, tailor shop, dressmaking shop, millinery store, doll factory as well as its own publishing house.

These money-making ventures were extremely profitable and bore a remarkable resemblance to the programmes in later years of the Nation of Islam. One thing is certain from this roll call of achievement – 1919 was a pivotal and productive year for the various Garvey enterprises.

UNIA

With the growth of its membership between 1918 and 1924, as well as income from its various economic enterprises the organisation purchased additional party Halls in the USA, Belize, Canada, Costa Rica, Jamaica, Panama and other countries. The UNIA also purchased farms in Ohio and other states.

By 1920 the association had over 1,100 divisions in more than 40 countries. Most divisions were located in the United States, which had become the UNIA's base of operations.

But there were also offices in several Caribbean countries, including Cuba – which had the most.

UNIA was well-represented across the British Empire with a presence in Nigeria, Ghana, South Africa and even Australia.

This led to a flurry of activity between different colonial governments trying to undermine the organisation and, especially, Garvey.

The first International UNIA convention was held during August 1920 at Madison Square Garden in New York with 20,000 members in attendance.

International UNIA convention 1920

The Convention ratified the Declaration of Negro Rights, and elected Garvey as the "Provisional President of Africa." This, of course, created major shockwaves in the USA and in Africa.

Amongst the other declarations was one proclaiming the red, black and green flag the official banner of the UNIA as well as a symbol representing the entire African race.

In later years, notably during the 1960's, the flag was adopted by Black nationalists and a new generation of Pan-Africanists as the Black Liberation Flag.

The convention was a clear announcement of the UNIA as a Black nationalist organisation seeking the upliftment of Africans, encouraging self-liberation.

The legacy of the different paths being followed by Du Bois and Garvey during the 1920s, who Padmore referred to in later years as "the two outstanding Negro leaders in the Western Hemisphere"[40], is still being felt today.

The increasingly socialist path being followed by Du Bois had three core principles. It believed in working-class unity as well as the need for Black workers to self-organise collectively. It also was a politics based on a fierce opposition to all forms of colonial rule.

The African nationalism espoused by Garvey, at least in his early days, was also anti-capitalist and anti-colonialist.

But Garvey unmistakably retreated from a radical perspective after the 1920 convention.

His nationalism, from then on, became aggressively separatist in its approach and encompassed a decidedly conservative self-reliance.

---

40. G. Padmore, 1955, p.106.

At the UNIA's convention in 1921 Garvey said:

"We sincerely feel that the white race like the black
and yellow races should maintain the purity of self
....[The negro] therefore denounces any attempt on
the part of dissatisfied individuals who by accident
are members of the said negro race, in their attempts
to foster a campaign of miscegenation to the
destruction of the race's purity".[41]

The rightward political shift by Garvey I believe reflects
a tension that exists in African diaspora politics today.

In simple terms is Marxism a "white man's thing," with
no real meaning for African workers? Or is it something
that can be used and adapted, as the scientific approach
that it represents towards developing a programme for
African liberation?

Marcus Garvey

---

41. RA Hill (ed), *The Marcus Garvey and UNIA Papers: Vols 1-5*. University of California
Press, Los Angeles, 1983.

Also the extent to which African workers should collaborate with white workers to resist racism and the wider exploitation facing all working people has always been and continues to be a great source of tension.

Self-liberation does not have to mean separatist. But, as we can see from this and earlier chapters, there must be a respect from white workers towards Africans that does not dismiss the particular everyday experience of racism that is faced within and outside the labour movement.

This points to the need for a de-colonisation of the theory and practice of the labour movement – something I will return to in the final chapter.

Later in the century another international movement emerged as the sun began to set on the old colonial rule. It was a movement that, for a period at least, gave hope to the vast majority of the people of the world.

The Non Aligned Movement

In 1955 delegates from 29 countries, representing 54 per cent of the world's population, gathered in Bandung, Indonesia, to sign a 10-point pledge against war and for the "promotion of mutual interests and cooperation," amongst what was actually by far the majority of the world's population.

The early leaders of the Non-Aligned Movement (NAM) were true political giants of the era. Africans Gamel Abdel Nasser of Egypt and Kwame Nkrumah of Ghana were key figures on the world stage alongside Indian leader Jawaharlal Nehru, Josef Broz Tito of Yugoslavia and Sukarno of Indonesia.

Even with the prominence of these leaders there still seems something rather strange in a gathering of people representing billions of people coming together to develop a united movement to throw off the shackles placed on them – even after colonialism – by a small but powerful elite.

But, the reality is, this represents the challenge that faces the working and peasant classes to this day.

The conference in Indonesia was the spark of a radical movement for change that – like the words of a school report – never really achieved its potential.

But it created a new spirit – the Bandung Spirit – where the global majority demanded that more priority should be paid to dealing with their welfare rather than the warfare threatened should a nuclear conflict break out between the US and the USSR.

This period was at the height of the Cold War when the Global South – then usually referred to as the Third World – were being forced to choose between one superpower or the other.

Whilst the Global South was emerging from colonialism into a new period of "notional" independence the creation of the NAM was not just a challenge to the US and the USSR that another way was possible off the back of the successful and soon to be successful liberation movement – it was also a challenge to what Vijay Prashad calls the "Darker Nations".

It is important to consider the role of the NAM in the international movement for African liberation. Not because all of the countries involved were African – because they were not. But because it allowed newly liberated Africans to act on a transnational basis in

a way that had never been possible since the brutal
transatlantic slave trade.

It did not end the ruthless exploitation of African
resources by the rich nations. The ruthless capitalists
simply ousted or killed anyone, such as Patrice
Lumumba or Thomas Sankara that was not prepared to
tow their line.

They also made sure that the proxy leaders they put in
place were able to gain unimaginable wealth while the
people of their nations struggled to survive.

But Bandung was a message that the freedom won from
colonialism in Africa and Asia heralded a refusal to be
dictated to by the superpowers.

Bandung conference

NAM really began to come into its own in 1961 when Tito hosted a heads of government meeting.

The focus of NAM in those early days focused on the need for further decolonisation, promoting nuclear disarmament and the anti-apartheid movement.

But NAM also prioritised developing unity between nations of the Global South and using this to temper the relationships between the US and the USSR.

NAM used this South solidarity to attack the way that capitalism was stacked against the Global South while the rich got richer off their backs.

Its harshest critics find it hard to ignore the importance of NAM during the 1960s through to the 1980s.

But once the so-called Washington consensus took a foothold during the 1980s so did the influence of NAM. The betrayal of the USSR in 1991 was a further nail in the coffin of NAM as the US took control of what has since become known as a "unipolar" world.

The NAM simply was not strong or cohesive enough to act as any real counterweight towards the hegemony of the US. NAM summits go by without being barely noticed these days.

Few media outlets feel the need to report on the declarations coming out of these largely talking shops.

In the meantime, African nations continue to be ruthlessly exploited for the rich natural resources they have, and are deliberately excluded from a seat at key decision-making tables – such as the United Nations Security Council.

But it begs the question as to whether a seat around a table that has no food in a house that is burning down around you is the height of African liberation ambition.

That is why we need a new approach and why new life must be given to a revamped non-aligned movement.

Without this Africa and its diaspora will continue to fall victim to the US Cold War mentality that continues to dominate geopolitics.

The peacemongers of the world need to be as organised and as determined as the war makers.

To help achieve this there needs to be a strong collective determined to place the interests of people over warfare. Nowhere is this more urgently needed than for the African continent.

Creating a new non-aligned movement from the remnants of the existing one is not as far-fetched as it might initially sound.

The G77 plus China group, which brings vast swathes of the Global South together shows that there is still an interest in shifting the paradigm of geopolitics away from the all-pervading interests of the US in favour of most of humanity.

In the final chapter I will look at the G77 plus China group along with other multilateral groups that have been critical in supporting, or at least, providing a platform for African communities of resistance.

Diego Campos/MCom, *Reunião anual de ministros das Comunicações do Brics*, 2023

CHAPTER FOUR
Laying a new Jericho Road

Introduction

I am not a Christian but the parable of the Good Samaritan (Luke 10: 25-37), which talks of a man travelling from Jerusalem to Jericho along the Jericho road has stuck with me since I heard it referred to in a speech by Rev Martin Luther King Jr many years ago.

The Jericho road was known as seventeen miles of violence and oppression. It was a dangerous road with many twists and turns and many places along the way where you can be easily ambushed by bandits.

It was a real place that until the fifth century was even called the red or bloody way where, up to the nineteenth century, travellers paid money to local warlords for safe passage.

Africans, whether on the continent or in the diaspora, need to construct a new Jericho road on which to travel. This may not resemble the old one or take the exact same route but it should learn from the past and build on existing theories, practices and structures to help find a new way forward towards freedom and liberation.

The chief world bandit appears to be the US who through its doctrine of full spectrum dominance will go to any lengths to maintain the power of monopoly capital – including through the use of direct warfare or through the use of proxy forces such as the Ukrainians.

This chapter offers a few thoughts on the way forward to break this US stranglehold but also to continue the unstoppable rise of the Global South and the central role played in it by Africans.

The African Continent

Institutions such as the African Union (AU) have, in the main, made little difference to the lives of the population of the continent.

Despite declarations, projects and programmes most Africans struggle just to survive amidst war, famine and the specific impacts of the climate emergency.

A deadly conflict was sparked in Sudan between the country's military and paramilitary forces in mid-April of 2023.

This, according to the United Nations, put the African nation on course to become the world's worst hunger crisis.

The genocide being inflicted on the Palestinians by the Israelis in Gaza and the Russian invasion of Ukraine has largely overshadowed this grave situation.

The AU has been completely powerless to do anything about the conflict or the fact that Africa is, and has been for some time, largely an extraction zone for the Global North.

Slavery, of the modern variety, is still a fact of life as young kids are forced to mine the massive mineral resources, such as cobalt and uranium, to name but two, that the Global North needs to maintain its wealth and power.

The AU seems comfortable in helping the rich and powerful nations to become even wealthier and ever more powerful at the expense of the African workers.

The AU also seems comfortable to provide a platform for the West's proxy leaders whilst, just in Sudan, around six million people face the real prospect of starvation.

The positive news is that there are countless grassroots self-liberation strategies across Africa that are not waiting for increasingly irrelevant bodies such as the African Union to make a difference.

The Economic Communities of West African States (ECOWAS) showed how completely irrelevant it was to what was happening on the ground when it failed to recognise the groundswell of public support for the military takeovers in the Sahel region.

It was forced to quietly drop its initial US and French prompted threat of military intervention when they realised the extent of popular support for removing the dictators they had been all too willing to support.

Local people were also supporting the seizing of power from the former colonial rulers and the US who had plundered the resources of these nations.

This shows the importance of removing the despots in Africa who work at the behest of the US and their posse.

The fact that Niger, until the military takeover one of the poorest nations in the world – despite its wealth in uranium and other precious minerals – is now one of the fastest growing economies in the world would not have gone unnoticed by other nations.

Institutions that do not serve the people must be discarded in favour of those that will. The AU and ECOWAS fall into this category.

New means of developing national and transnational African power must be found.

The Rise of the Brics

Brics – the bloc named for its five original members – Brazil, Russia, India, China and South Africa – is a body that will be critical to the future rise of Africa.

In 2024 five new nations were admitted to membership – Egypt, Ethiopia, Iran, Saudi Arabia and the United Arab Emirates. But more than 40 other countries want to be part of this exciting project.

Before the new additions Brics already had a cumulative Gross Domestic Product of around $28 trillion – something like a 26 per cent share of global GDP. The new members add something in the region of another $3 trillion.

Brics nations already represent around half of the world's population.

The rise of the Brics nations is clearly a symptom of a deeper malaise. The default position of the US and its posse of fellow colonial powers to slap sanctions on anyone who fails to tow the line is not unnoticed across the Global South. Why would it? Nations of the Global South are often the victims of this US reflex position towards anyone that fails to agree with its latest line.

West's proclivity to deploy unilateral financial sanctions, abuse international payments mechanisms, renege on climate finance commitments, and accord scant respect to food security and health imperatives of the Global South during the pandemic are only some of the elements responsible for the growing disenchantment with the prevailing international system.

The expansion of the Brics is more than just a rise in the number of people joining a club. It has a much greater political, economic and social significance.

Brics has many echoes of the "Spirit of Bandung" in the way that has caught the imagination of a Global South sick to death with being ordered around by the US.

A Global South fed up with being told what it can do and who it is permissible to have relationships with without facing crippling economic sanctions.

Talk of the creation of new financial arrangements based on mutuality or "win-win" and non-interference in the domestic affairs is critical for Africa and the rest of the Global South.

Brics appears ready to find ways to challenge the dollar as the world's reserve currency. Trading in sovereign currencies rather than through the almighty dollar is already becoming a reality.

The massive 2023 rupee-designated oil transaction between India and the United Arab Emirates is more than a swipe at the petrodollar arrangement that has governed since 1973.

It also signals to others that the world does not come to an end by not using the dollar and that other financial arrangements are possible that do not allow the US to continue to slap sanctions on any country that fails to do exactly as they are told by the White House.

This is, in reality, should it develop, a path away from financial subservience for African nations who can become free to avoid the Jericho road populated by the US bandits.

Brics will hopefully not develop into a military alliance. This is certainly not the intention that is being put forward.

The aim seems to be to break away from the hegemony of US rule.

The truth is that African nations, in common with the rest of the Global South, will remain under the boot of the US unless these new arrangements can be made on the basis of non-interference in domestic affairs.

There must be mutual respect in international relations – something sadly lacking from the US, the Group of seven gang, the European Union and the military wing of these allies, NATO.

The Brics vision is for a greater voice for Global South in world affairs, as South African President Cyril Ramaphosa said at the 2023 summit when recalling the Bandung Conference of 1955.

BRICS conference

It is highly likely that more African and Caribbean nations will soon expand the ranks of the Brics to exert their own right to sovereignty that the US and its allies are all too quick to assert for the likes of Ukraine but which they clearly have never thought applied to the "darker nations."

Brics does not overshadow the role of the largely Global South dominated Group of 77 plus China nations.

As Brics develops this body will continue to play an important role. But as that development gains pace and more nations join it will be interesting to see what role there will be for the G77 plus China group.

United Nations

Dag Hammarskjold, the tragic second United Nations secretary general, once said the organisation "was created not to lead mankind to heaven but to save humanity from hell".

Of course this depends very much on what kind of hell you had in mind.

The hell for Africans has appeared ceaseless with virtually no assistance from the UN.

The UN was set up to entrench US dominance.

The US saw itself as the predominant world power and was treated like that by most of the world, only the USSR and later through the NAM challenged that notion.

It has been prepared to unleash its own version of hell whenever and however they wanted to enforce that dominance.

Hammarskjold must have known that the UN was completely powerless to reign in the US and they could, and usually do pretty much anything that they want on the world stage.

The UN is, and has been for some time, a fairly ineffectual institution that merely acts as a useful idiot when the White House decides it has some role to perform in protecting US interests.

The proxy war being conducted by the US against Russia in Ukraine and the ramping up of tensions against China, and of course, its complete inability to do anything to stop the genocide in Gaza shows that there is no meaningful sign of life at the UN.

In Gaza the UN played no role whatsoever in talks aimed at bringing about a peaceful solution to the crisis.

The UN, based in the belly of the beast itself in New York, is a body devoid of any worthwhile criticism of the US.

Africa and African diasporic nations are treated as worse than second-class participants in the UN. They have no permanent seat on the main body, the Security Council, and are largely ignored or bullied by the US to vote its way at sessions of the General Assembly.

China and Brazil appear to be the only major nations making efforts to bring about peace in Ukraine and it was the Chinese who brought Saudi Arabia and Iran together to broker a deal to end the nearly eight-year-old conflict in Yemen. The UN failed.

The UN is reduced to being a conference organiser and to sending out press releases that are largely begging letters for more funding on important issues such as the climate emergency, water and a range of other issues.

Africa is largely discussed in terms of wars and famine but little else.

We need new global architecture that breaks away from US control.

The US dominance of the UN must be broken. The Security Council must have more than one permanent seat for the vast continent of Africa and it needs to hold representation for the African diaspora.

The African diaspora on the Caribbean islands rarely get a mention because the US, patronisingly, considers the region to be its "backyard." Yet it is an important region its own right where the African people present deserve to be allowed to shape their own destiny.

The region has consistently demanded the lifting of sanctions against Cuba and spoken forcefully for that to happen. But the UN system does not allow its annual decision in favour of Cuba to be binding on the US.

This must change. Without that the UN continues to operate as a useful idiot for the US to use or ignore at its will.

Brazil has the second largest population of Africans in the world after Nigeria.

This on its own should demand a permanent seat on the UN Security Council but so should the need to recognise the importance of the South American nation as one of the guardians of the lungs of the planet – the Amazon.

If the safeguarding of the Amazon is not a security issue for the world – as the climate emergency bites and conflicts over water and other essential for life become more frequent – then it is difficult to see what is.

The same can be said for both the International
Monetary Fund and the World Bank, both of which
exist to support the growth of profits for US-controlled
monopoly capital.

These bodies must also face radical reform and be broken
away from US dominance with far more accountability to
Africa and the nations of the Global South.

The shortcomings of the UN and the other major global
bodies and the lack of any respect they show to the
Global South has sparked a headlong rush to find new
ways to do business.

African nations and many countries of the Global
South are now seeing much more value in creating new
structures that take their interests into account – not just
as pawns of the US. Change is increasingly being seen
as the preferred route rather than slow and meaningless
reform as we can see with the direction being taken
through the Brics block.

The UN is a vital body for bringing today the nations
of the world but it is essentially the plaything of the US
and has already lost what little legitimacy it still has to
Africans across the globe.

Decolonising the labour movement

This book has sought to chart the role that Africans
have played in the resistance to racism and the rise of the
Global South.

It has also shown that the practice of building
communities of resistance at local, national and
international levels have been critical to this resistance.

It has never been resistance without a purpose.

Africans on the continent and in the diaspora have continued to develop their own pathways towards freedom from exploitation and the creation of a better world.

Many have wanted that world to be a socialist one while others have taken a more conservative or nationalistic viewpoint that has centred on becoming rich Africans – even at the expense of other Africans.

I think the world is at a critical point where the political grounds are shifting.

By the end of the decade the far right could well be voted into control of large swathes of the world.

The left needs to take up this challenge and build the widest level of unity possible which specifically includes women and people of African and Asian descent.

We need to plan our own new world order that brings together the majority of the world to break the dominance of the small ruling elite.

That is why African freedom alongside the liberation of working and peasant communities across the globe is so important.

But we will not be able to do this without being self-critical and understanding our own shortcomings as a movement.

Although less than 10 per cent of the world population are members of a trade union it is still a vital area for us to build.

Part of this decades-long decline has been because of the destruction by the capitalist class of the traditional work arenas where trade unionism was strong – for example in the heavy industrial sectors – and the creation of more insecure employment – sometimes called the gig economy.

But for Africans in most of the world, their experience is of relying on the informal economy to make a living.

Socialists need to support efforts to reach out into Africa's informal economy to build cadres that can break people out of their daily survival modes into understanding the importance of the sort of communities of resistance discussed throughout this book.

We can learn a lot from the Communist Party of India (Marxist) in this regard - especially through their work with agricultural workers.

Priority should be given to how this can be done.

But in the formal sector we should still look on an international level to deepen the class analysis and struggle of trade unions.

Uniquely amongst trade union organisations the Public Services International global union body has produced a pioneering piece of work that activists and theorists should all sit up and take note of.

In 2023 PSI published a document called *Decolonising Labour Regimes*.[42]

The document pointed out that: "Contemporary forms of racism, racial discrimination, xenophobia and related intolerance have their roots in slavery, colonialism and imperialism, which sought the denial of social, political,

42. Public Services International, *Decolonising Labour Regimes*, digital, 2023

and economic rights according to race, class, caste, gender, sexuality and geography in order to advance the European capitalist imperialist project.

"In addition to seizing control over natural resources in vast swathes of the world, Western imperialism sought to gain control over human labour, through slavery and when slavery was abolished, through other means of controlling and ensuring access to cheap and often forced or coerced labour on a massive scale."

The document goes on to say that addressing the root causes of racism "needs an understanding of the historical and contemporary relationship between capital, the construction of racial (and other) hierarchies and capital's imperative to control labour for the purposes of profit and wealth accumulation."

The report argues that racial capitalism is at the heart of racism across the globe.

The brilliant academic Ruth Wilson Gilmore explains that "racial capitalism, which is to say all capitalism, is not a thing, it's a relation.

"However, if we look back through the history of capitalism as it developed, we see that the understanding that those who own the means of production had their differences from those whose labour they exploited were understandings that we can recognise today as racial practice."

She added: "So, all capitalism is racial from its beginning—which is to say the capitalism that we have inherited, that is constantly producing and reproducing itself—and it will continue to depend on racial practice and racial hierarchy, no matter what. This is another way of saying we can't undo racism without undoing capitalism."[43]

R. Wilson Gilmore

This clarity is important - especially coming in a document from a trade union body that has been dominated in recent times by a conservative British trade union leader.

That these comments can appear in such a trade union document means that socialist trade unionists need to organise to go out and turn the theory into practice.

Key to this will be to ensure that we do not continue to engage in a competition to see which oppression facing the working class is more important than another.

Far too often this conceals a desire to do nothing.

43. R. Wilson Gilmore in Public Services International, Decolonising Labour Regimes, December 2023, https://publicservices.international/resources/digital-publication/decolonising-labour-regimes?id=14234&lang=en , accessed 2 May 2024.

Racism is systemic and so only system-wide change is appropriate.

Although this book has concentrated on manifestations and impacts of racism, the global system of racism makes us all poorer and has never been something that should be left to Africans to deal with.

I argue throughout this book that Africans have and must continue to take the lead in fighting racism but this should not be a lonesome affair which white people treat as a spectator sport.

To do this we must end the myth that anti African racism is a thing of the past or that things are somehow improving. For most people of African descent, wherever they are across the globe, the opposite is in fact true.

The global military industrial complex and the continued exploitation of Africans as cheap and "throw away" labour has become normalised and merely allowing a few Africans to seep through into positions of influence or even power does not alter this fact.

African women face the brunt of human rights abuses across the world and face a toxic brew of racism, misogyny and class exploitation that has largely been ignored by the labour movement of the Global North.

To tackle this the labour movement must stop conflating its vital and often impressive anti-colonial activism with anti-racism. Whilst belonging to the same family they are not the same.

The Global North labour movement, particularly the Marxists within it, also need to face up to its own "chauvinism" and not take it as a personal slight whenever this is pointed out but, instead, recognise the opportunity to develop our political analysis and use that to turn theory into practice.

Racism, xenophobia, homophobia, and misogyny are not the sole preserve of the right wing or of the capitalist class.

This book has shown time and time again when white activists have proved wanting when they were called upon to support African workers fighting against racism.

There are many and very notable exceptions to this which other books must demonstrate but we must tackle what many in the Black community, African and Asian, have often seen as an unchallenged internalised chauvinism of the left.

Solidarity in the struggle against racism is critical but it can not be unconditional. We simply cannot allow the racism that we claim to be fighting against that are often deeply ingrained into the subconscious to go unchallenged and to hinder our struggle for socialism.

This is a challenge to all of us who want to defeat capitalism and move towards socialism and if we are to achieve an African Uhuru.

Testimonials

"From the moment I met Roger more than 20 years ago, his brilliance and love for community was evident. A seasoned activist and leader whose passion for human rights, justice and fairness was obvious. Coming from a strong West Indian family himself, he understands the pride and how the trials and tribulations faced, can impact their strong sense of independence. As a trade union leader he often called upon and used examples of this ancestral history of resistance. After all it is this education and demand for justice, respect and equity/fairness that will eventually create a better world for all."

–Marie Clarke Walker
leading black Canadian trade unionist and community activist

"McKenzie's voice is a vital one to be added to the decolonisation and the 'reteaching' that Black British people have contributed to the fabric of society not just in the UK, but the global community. McKenzie's life of activism, campaigning consistently for visibility and equality for Black and intersectional communities determines his 360 view and voice is one of expertise, grounded in experience and passion."

–Michelle Codrington Rogers
Teacher and first Black national officer, NASUWT– the teachers union

"A giant of the anti-racist and labour movement spanning countless decades, Roger's first-hand experience helps weave together the stories of race & class & how communities of resistance were forged through struggle."

–Asad Rehman
The Executive Director of War on Want

manifesto
manifestopress.coop